Love Worth Finding

Love Worth Finding

THE LIFE OF ADRIAN ROGERS
AND HIS PHILOSOPY OF PREACHING

JOYCE ROGERS

with Julie-Allyson Ieron

BROADMAN
&HOLMAN
PUBLISHERS

NASHVILLE, TENNESSEE

Ten-Digit ISBN: 0805440755
Thirteen-Digit ISBN: 9780805440751

Published by Broadman & Holman Publishers
Nashville, Tennessee

Dewey Decimal Classification: B
Subject Heading: ROGERS, ADRIAN P. \
CLERGY—BIOGRAPHY \ PREACHING

Unless otherwise noted, all Scripture is taken from the King James
Version.

Scripture quotations marked NKJV are taken from the New King James
Version, copyright © 1979, 1980, 1982, Thomas Nelson, Inc., Publishers.

Scripture citations marked HCSB are taken from the *Holman Christian
Standard Bible*® Copyright © 1999, 2000, 2002, 2004 by Holman Bible
Publishers. Used by permission.

1 2 3 4 5 6 7 8 9 10   10 09 08 07 06 05

ACKNOWLEDGEMENTS

This volume is sent out with great appreciation and dedication to those who helped make it possible.

While this is not an autobiography as such, my wife and beloved sweetheart took notes as we traveled and talked together. This book would not be a reality without her labor of love, and I dedicate it to her, the one who has helped me live for Jesus through the years and has helped me chronicle His blessings.

Also, I wish to thank Dr. Dennis Brunet for allowing me to quote freely from the doctoral dissertation he did on my philosophy of preaching. I owe him a great debt.

Next, I wish to acknowledge Julie-Allyson Ieron for her tireless effort to get this work edited in time for my retirement celebration. Julie, you have worked "under the gun" and have gone the second mile. I am deeply grateful.

Also, I want to say thank you to Ruth Ann Shelton, a dear friend, who loaned her special talent to us by helping arrange photographic material in the center of this book.

I want to acknowledge my faithful administrative assistant, Linda Glance, for researching some of the historical details in this book.

Next, I wish to thank the dear friends at Broadman & Holman Publishers. I'm grateful for Ken Stephens, who first floated the idea, and to Len Goss, senior editor, who guided us through. Thank you gentlemen. You are the greatest!

Last, but most important of all, I sincerely want to give honor and praise to the dear Savior. I would be a sheer fool not to recognize and be grateful for His hand upon my life. I've made many mistakes, but the Lord never gave up on me. The victories described in this book belong to Jesus. Praise His name!

CONTENTS

FOREWORD

On hearing that Adrian Rogers announced his retirement from Bellevue Baptist Church to devote himself to his media ministry, to teaching at Mid-America Theological Seminary, and to the Adrian Rogers Pastor Training Institute, my remorse was ameliorated somewhat by the announcement that this biography and philosophy of preaching would be forthcoming. Even for those of us fortunate enough to have walked through the mountains and valleys of life in close proximity to the spiritual colossus whose life is chronicled in the volume, few know the whole story of this remarkable duo, Joyce and Adrian Rogers.

This book is more than the story of a prophet of God. Here is the invigorating account of a family—husband and father, wife and mother, children and grandchildren. It is the story of five church families, how they shaped a prophet, and what blessings these congregations garnered as they sat enthralled under this extraordinary preacher, who, like a Florida sloop, caught the wind of the Spirit in his sails and thundered with his resonant voice from behind the sacred desk like the collapsing black clouds in an Atlantic sea squall.

Someone might ask how it is possible to combine biography with a philosophy of preaching. This volume answers that question: a preacher's biography is about nothing if not about preaching, while the philosophy of preaching is that which has been hammered out on the anvil of Adrian Rogers' mind for thirty-two years of faithful proclamation at Bellevue. For example, Rogers insists that conversion or the new birth is essential to effective preaching, observing, "You cannot preach what you do not know any more than you can come from where you have not been."

His own vivid experience with the living Christ accounts not only for the success of Adrian Rogers but also for his faith, courage, steadfastness, passion, and compassion.

All of these qualities are clearly apparent in Rogers' work behind the sacred desk.

Observers of eloquent preachers who have achieved prominence through pulpit and church often see these pulpiteers as bigger than life. Gifted with a handsome, athletic physique and a deep, resonant voice, which, when raised to a shout, could cause chairs to wobble like a gyroscope, Rogers seems to have it all together.

But the Rogers family portrayed in this volume served in small churches as well as a megachurch. They knew relative poverty, endured abuses at the hands of those who considered them radical, and plumbed the depths of sorrow in the loss of a precious baby boy.

Rogers was not born to denominational or ecclesiastical aristocracy. From unobtrusive origins, he rose to become the most prominent among Southern Baptist preachers. Within the Southern Baptist Convention, even before the passing of W. A. Criswell, the mantle of the latter had fallen comfortably around the shoulders of the high-school quarterback from Palm Beach, Fla. At the same time his rhetorical excellence was sought eagerly even beyond the Southern Baptist Zion. Invited by more than one United States president to come to the White House, Rogers emerged as one of the best and most widely loved leaders in evangelical Christendom.

To the outside world, a man with the stature of Adrian Rogers towers like a lone pine tree on a solitary mountain. The reality is that a retinue of lives form the matrix out of which the lofty tree has grown. To meet the men whose lives and ministries shaped the grandeur of the tree is a fascinating encounter. Rogers speaks of these at some length. No less intriguing are the early exploits of Rogers as a youthful preacher demonstrating early many of the qualities that later blossomed into an international leader. Imagine the embarrassment of the critic who opined about Adrian, "That boy will never make a preacher."

For preachers especially, just to have Rogers' philosophy of preaching is worth the investment in the book. Here you are invited to slip into a chair in the preacher's study and learn what motivates and guides the master preacher. Then you walk with him onto the platform and stand in his shoes as he addresses sinners as well as saints. You'll experience with him poignant moments, such as the physical attack on him during a sermon at Bellevue.

Rogers' admiration for Vance Havner is exhibited in his similar mastery of the epigram and the turn of a phrase. Expressions, such as "A preacher will milk many cows but churn his own butter," abound in the book as they do in his preaching and conversation.

Thoughts offered the reader regarding the future of preaching should greatly encourage even the most timid preachers. Often there are insights uncommon to other treatises on homiletics, such as the discussion of the role and critical importance of the congregation in preaching. This section of the book is vintage Adrian.

Only a few times in any century does a man rise out of the ranks of the ordinary with a touch of God upon him in such a way as to change the course of all human history. Further, for that man to be a man of impeccable moral standards, while possessing a pastor's heart, remarkable alacrity, profound dedication to the work of the Savior, as well as matchless pulpit eloquence and brilliance is extraordinary.

To say that this is exactly what God gave the world in Adrian Rogers is not an attempt to fell the oak of his humility, but only to recognize what most of us know is true in order to praise God for what He has done through him and to thank Adrian Rogers for allowing God to have the use of all of his talents and abilities.

PAIGE PATTERSON, PRESIDENT
SOUTHWESTERN BAPTIST THEOLOGICAL SEMINARY
FORT WORTH, TEXAS

DEDICATED TO MY SWEETHEART

I cannot imagine life without Joyce. She is my first-time—all time Sweetheart. I first set my eyes on her in the fourth grade. Later in the sixth grade she sat six desks in front of me to my right side. I was fascinated by her. During this period of time I would walk her home from school. Though she was not upset with me, she made a statement while we were walking, "I hate boys!" At that I made up my mind that I would change her opinion. From time to time I would drop a "love note" by her desk. Obviously, she didn't hate boys as much as she said, because she still has and treasures those notes. Our childhood friendship grew into another stage that is sometimes called "puppy love." But both puppies liked it. By the time we were in high school we knew that we were in love and that it was the real thing. We were both growing in our spiritual faith and our affinity for each other. While I played football in high school, Joyce was a cheerleader. One of my treasures is an autographed picture from Joyce in her cheerleader outfit. (They were more modest in those days.) She had written, "I'll always cheer you on," and indeed she has. We were married after our first year in college. Our marriage has sometimes known hardship, sorrow and minor disagreements, but I can honestly say it has been a magnificent marriage. On our wedding night we reaffirmed our love to Jesus and gave Him our marriage to guard and bless.

Most of our time together will be chronicled in this book, so I will bring this part to a conclusion. But let me say a word about the influence Joyce has been on my life. She has been a confidant, encourager, prayer partner, companion, and lover through the years. My love for her has not diminished but has been enhanced with each successive year. Joyce has not failed to admonish and correct me when it has been needed, yet she has done it with a respectful spirit.

Does all of this seem too serious? You would not think so if you could hear the laughter that rings through our home. We have played together as well as prayed together. Not only have we laughed together but we have enjoyed friends, family, travel, and adventure that have been the source of genuine joy, because Jesus has been at the center of it all. It is without exaggeration when I say that Joyce has been the dominant influence for good in my life and in our family.

I love you, Joyce

Adrian

NOTES AND TRIBUTE FROM AN ADORING WIFE

I want to tell you the story of how this book came to be. A young seminary student, Dennis Brunet, wrote my husband ten years ago asking if he could interview him in preparation for his doctoral dissertation at New Orleans Baptist Theological Seminary on the life and preaching of Adrian Rogers. One segment of this extensive dissertation dealt with questions that Dennis Brunet asked Adrian in a personal interview.

When the project was finished, Dennis and his wife came to Memphis and had lunch with Adrian and me. He brought a bound copy of his dissertation and presented it to my husband as a gift. He told us he hoped we would pursue having it published.

Reticent about pursuing such a project about himself, Adrian read the manuscript and packed it away.

Fast forward ten years. While Adrian was recovering from an illness, I remembered the book. He found it, and I began to read it aloud to him. The more I read, the more it gripped me that this work should be published for others to read.

The dissertation majored on preaching and told only a little about Adrian's life and ministry. So we began to reminisce through the years. When we went out in the car together, I would take a yellow legal pad and write down the events as they unfolded in our memory. Some were serious, some were sad, others were humorous or momentous. We began to look forward to these trips as we remembered the highlights of our lives and ministry.

Then someone from Broadman & Holman Publishers got in touch and said they would be interested in doing a biography or autobiography of Adrian's life and ministry. It dawned on us that perhaps this is why we had been impressed to remember and write these events at this time.

In the pages that follow, we have included both our personal experiences and a portion of the material gathered for the dissertation. As you read this portion of the book, please keep in mind that Adrian answered the interviewer's questions extemporaneously; we edited his answers little. The extemporaneous answers are more effective because they represent the overflow of Adrian's experience in ministry and proclamation of the Word. These are not carefully crafted thoughts that have been formally prepared at a desk but rather expressions out of his heart of concerns and beliefs worked out on the anvil of experience.

Now I would like to pay tribute to this man whom I have known since I was a child. I still treasure the love notes he dropped by my desk in the sixth grade. He is my one and only sweetheart. I can't imagine life without Adrian. He has been a courageous man ever since I can remember. First, he exhibited this courage on the football field. Then as he stood for the truth and for what was right—even when it might cost his reputation. I have always been proud to be married to this courageous man.

He's the only pastor I've had since I married him fifty-three years ago. He has been my chief discipler as he has broken the bread of life and fed my soul week after week, year after year. I've never heard him preach a boring sermon. He is a mighty expositor of the Word of God. I love God's Word more because of him.

He also has been a fun-loving man. He loves to laugh. One night when I got up, he decided to have some fun and put his head under the cover and his feet on the pillow. When I got back into bed, I turned and kissed his foot. It worked just like he planned. We probably laughed for twenty minutes. He can tell a joke on any subject I can name. He draws illustrations from all of life's experiences. He loves to recite poetry and will delight me with these choice tidbits that he has learned down through the years.

Many nights before we go to sleep, he will ask me to name a subject. When I do, he then begins to weave a creative tale, entertaining me until we nod off to sleep. He has told me many stories about "The Adventures of Wanda and Wilbur Woostie," an imaginary couple who have lived exciting and adventurous lives.

He gave me a little bear for Valentine's Day many years ago that said on it, "This bears my love." That bear has traveled around the world, appearing on many surprise occasions. The most creative appearance was in the office of the Mayor of Moscow, Russia, when Adrian persuaded the Vice-Mayor to walk across the room to present me the "love bear."

For many years our funds and furnishings were limited because we chose to have children before we had things. But on our forty-fifth wedding anniversary Adrian took me on "the trip of a lifetime" to what I consider to be the most beautiful place in the world—the mountains and lakes of Switzerland. We've now been married fifty-three years, and he's taken me back to this beautiful country several times.

On beautiful Mt. Rigi, outside of Lucerne, Switzerland, he "instituted" this delightful tradition—"the casting of the flowers," where we pick a bouquet of wild flowers and toss them over the mountain's edge one at a time, labeling each flower with a quality we love about the other person.

During the early years of our marriage, I stayed home most of the time with the children. Now I am able to go with him to minister for the Lord in many parts of the world. As long as the Lord gives me strength, I'm going to be right by his side.

After wrestling with the decision for over two years, he recently offered his retirement as pastor of our beloved Bellevue Baptist Church. He has been a pastor for fifty-three years and at Bellevue thirty-two of those years. But he desires to hand the baton over to God's new man and bless him to continue the race at Bellevue.

In the days ahead we want to pursue a ministry of sharing with younger pastors and wives what God has taught us and encouraging them to faithfully run the race. He is determined to be faithful and to finish well!

Adrian, you'll always be the one I love,

Joyce

PART ONE

THE LIFE AND MINISTRY OF ADRIAN ROGERS

CHAPTER

1

EARLY YEARS AND FAMILY BACKGROUND

Sixteen-year old Adrian Rogers had already gone to bed when he heard his father and a close family friend sitting on the patio just outside his bedroom window having a conversation. The friend asked, "What is Adrian going to do with his life?"

"He wants to be a preacher," Adrian's father replied.

The friend laughed and said, "That boy will never make a preacher."

This wasn't the first time others had cast doubts on the future of this young man. In junior high school Adrian was known to be unruly and belligerent. He had an overdose of courage and the ability to fight with his fists. He had gained a reputation of being one the toughest kids in school. He would challenge others to a fight just for an expression of what must have been an inner turmoil. He had challenged his classmates one by one to a dual of fisticuffs. Some would surrender without a fight. The others were prodded into conflict.

Not only this, but early on he developed bad habits in language and personal integrity. He would "borrow" answers on a test from a person near him. Truancy was a regular occurrence that he covered up with phony excuses.

Adrian kept most of this side of his life a secret from me, and I knew him at a different level. His teachers, however, and the principal of the junior high school were not in the dark about this trouble-making student. Ironically, the principal of Northboro Junior High School contacted my mother and warned her that her daughter was keeping company with the "meanest boy in school."

When Adrian turned fourteen, he yielded his life to Jesus and a radical transformation took place. It was so vivid that teachers began to ask, "What happened to Adrian? He is so changed." That change was real and has lasted for sixty years.

Adrian often has said that if it were not for Jesus and His transforming grace that he would not be a nice person to live with and may have even ended up in prison. In retrospect, he feels that he would have come to Christ at an earlier age if someone had shared the gospel with him.

While God indeed did make a preacher out of Adrian, it was not without some deep pain and sorrow. Adrian and I were molded and fashioned on the anvil of a great loss.

Tragedy on Mother's Day

Just three weeks after Adrian and I arrived at our first church out of seminary, tragedy struck our little family. It was on Mother's Day. After lunch was finished and the children were put to bed for their naps, I was headed for the bedroom to take a nap. I stopped by little Philip's crib to check on him and he looked strange. I called for Adrian to come quickly and horrified asked, "Is he dead?"

Adrian quickly picked up his little body and tucked him inside his coat. He told me to stay there because the other children were asleep, and he did not want to alarm them.

He drove as quickly as he could to the hospital. The attendant took the baby from his arms and rushed to see what they could do.

Unashamedly, Adrian fell to his knees in the hospital corridor and cried out to God for help. But the doctor returned to sadly report, "I'm sorry, son. He's gone." Later, Philip's death was diagnosed as Sudden Infant Death Syndrome (SIDS).

Adrian returned home, and I saw him coming up the front walk empty handed. I knew in my heart that Philip was gone to be with Jesus.

We called our family and a few church members to tell them about Philip's death. The word spread swiftly throughout the small congregation, and people began to come to the house to express their condolences.

They put their arms and their love around us. This began a bonding that never ceased. Soon our parents arrived. We gathered a few belongings and began our journey to our hometown, West Palm Beach, which was just an hour away. Steve and Gayle, ages 4 and 2, rode with their grandparents, giving us an opportunity to reflect on this sadness that had suddenly invaded our lives.

We were living next to the church at this time, so as we pulled out of the driveway that Sunday evening, the church services were just beginning. The windows of the church building were open, and we could hear the congregation singing.

> No, never alone ! No, never alone!
> He promised never to leave me
> Never to leave me alone.

Truly, this was a message from God to us. Then as we drove toward "home," we reflected on the death of our infant son and sang songs that God brought to our minds. The song we especially remembered was Joseph Scriven's emotive lyric, "What a Friend We Have in Jesus."

> What a friend we have in Jesus
> All our sins and griefs to bear;
> What a privilege to carry
> Everything to God in prayer.
>
> Oh, what peace we often forfeit
> Oh, what needless pain we bear;
> All because we do not carry
> Everything to God in prayer.

Can we find a friend so faithful
Who will all our sorrows share?
Jesus knows our every weakness
Take it to the Lord in prayer.

We continued to sing all the way home. God used the messages of these hymns to comfort our saddened hearts. The following days seemed like a dream as we made preparations for the funeral. We decided on a meaningful grave marker. It would read, "Philip!" "Yes, Lord!" The message was clear. God had called our little son, and he had answered that call.

I can still recall the pain I felt as I stood at Philip's grave. But then, I sensed the assurance of God speaking to my heart, "He's not there. He's up here with Me!"

After the funeral Pastor Allan Watson took me by the arm. As he led me away, he counseled me to take the love I had for Philip and pour it into the lives of the children I still had. That evening at my parents' home, everyone else had gone to bed early, leaving us alone in the living room. As Steve and Gayle played in the living room, I remembered the pastor's words. A great gratitude for them came over me. That is what I would do—continue to love and care for these two gifts from God.

Although the death of our infant son was devastating, it was not defeating. Adrian and I cast ourselves on the Lord in a way we had never done before. Jesus became the greater focus of our lives, and we began to realize more than ever His total sufficiency.

The following week Adrian was in the hospital visiting a man to whom he had been witnessing. That man asked, "Are you still serving God after what He did to you?"

Adrian replied, "Of course I am. Had there been no sin, there would have been no sickness and death. Sin came into the world through Satan. He was the initiator of sin, and Jesus is the only answer. I'm not going to line up with the Devil. Satan's got a bigger enemy than he's ever had. Jesus is the only answer to sin and suffering."

Adrian recalls,

> I also remember on that devastating day, shortly after
> Philip's death, I found a verse that seemed to be God's
> direct word in this dark hour. It was found in 2 Corinthians
> 1:3-4, "Blessed be God, even the Father of our Lord Jesus
> Christ, the Father of mercies, and the God of all comfort;
> Who comforteth us in all our tribulation, that we may be
> able to comfort them which are in any trouble, by the
> comfort wherewith we ourselves are comforted of God."
>
> Joyce and I determined to be good stewards of our
> sorrow and to comfort others with the comfort that we
> had experienced. This comfort was the presence of the
> living Christ within us. It was a truth that became more
> real in our experience day by day.

We learned while talking with others who are experiencing grief that
it is not our responsibility to meet this person's need but to introduce
them to the only One Who is the ultimate answer. All good counsel
brings the individual to an encounter with and a surrender to the Lord
Jesus Christ.

We made an effort to focus our hearts on Jesus instead of our grief.
Also, we gave up to the Lord our so-called right to understand why this
happened and began to praise Him by faith. Going deeper into God's
Word and finding strength from specific promises brought great peace in
the midst of our storm.

We have endeavored to live by these principles and share them with
others. Men throw broken things away, but it seems that God never uses
anything until He first breaks it.

These and other experiences God used to deepen and mature Adrian's
faith. God did make a preacher out of him and has allowed him to serve
three terms as president of the Southern Baptist Convention, the world's

largest Protestant denomination. It did not seem that this bashful boy would pastor a megachurch and be heard by millions on radio and television around the world.

Family Background

Adrian Pierce Rogers was born September 12, 1931, in West Palm Beach, Fla., the third child of Arden and Rose Rogers. He describes his parents as "good, hard working salt-of-the-earth kind of people." They were a middle class family who had moved from Georgia to Florida shortly before the Great Depression of 1929. Although not financially affluent, they did create a stable home environment. Adrian says of them:

> My father became an orphan at age ten and was passed around, living with one relative, then another, doing hard farm work. Although my father and mother had little formal education, they had innate abilities.
>
> I remember my father as a diligent and affable man who always dressed "snappy," kept his shoes highly polished and played as hard as he worked.
>
> He had natural leadership qualities that caused him to rise to the top and excel in whatever task he undertook. He had a resonant baritone voice that was passed down to me and has been a great help in my calling as a preacher.
>
> My mother, although limited in her education, read widely and could discourse on almost any subject.
>
> She had a quick wit and a story that would embellish almost every conversation. I think I see traces of these characteristics in my own life that have served me in the ministry.

His mother and father loved children—especially their children. Adrian's older sister, Alliean, became a nurse and then an interior decorator. His older brother Arden, known as Buddy, became an electrical engineer and his younger brother, Barry, became comptroller of a college.

Akie and Buddy

Adrian and Arden, known at that time as Akie and Buddy, played a lot of boyhood pranks. One time Buddy placed his head under the house with his body lying out on the ground. They buried Adrian's body in the sand and cut out a hole in a newspaper close to his head and put catsup around it to look like blood. Then they placed a machete nearby to make it look like his head had been cut off. Someone then called their mother to come quickly. As she was looking at this awful scene, Adrian winked at her.

Akie and Buddy also spent many happy hours in their canvas-covered kayak propelled by an ancient 3.5 horsepower Johnson outboard motor. One day the two boys left the saltwater lagoon called Lake Worth and made their way in their little boat through the inlet into the vast Atlantic Ocean, although their father had warned the boys never to venture into the ocean in their fragile craft. To make the deed all the more foolish, the Coast Guard had put up small-craft warnings that day because of high wind and enormous waves. The father and the Coast Guard were right, and the boys were wrong. Adrian recalls:

> When the boat capsized, I remember looking up at a monstrous translucent wave and the sunlight showing through it. It came crashing into the boat, filling it with icy water. The little motor gave a hissing sound and stopped running. The tackle went to the bottom along with an overcoat I had brought along.
>
> Another vicious wave swept away the life preservers we were sitting on. The boat had no flotation and normally would have sunk. But as it turned over, it captured some air that kept it afloat.

My brother and I are strong swimmers. We held to the
boat and with kicking motions pushed it to the shore.
There it rolled over and over and was destroyed by the
beating surf. We borrowed a match from a fisherman
nearby and built a bonfire because we were shivering with
cold. But we both felt God had delivered us.

It was a long walk home that day for two young men
who had learned a lesson we would never forget.

Some years later as a "boy preacher," Adrian used this story as an
illustration, while preaching in the church where he and Buddy had grown
up. He told the story carefully and accurately, with great dramatic effect.
He made the point that some lives are shipwrecked by disobedience. To
punctuate the point Adrian said, "I believe I was saved in order to preach
the gospel. I don't know why God saved my brother."

When the congregation roared with laughter, the young preacher felt
he had ruined it all and felt humiliated. But that night there was a mighty
moving of God's Spirit and a number of people gave their hearts to Jesus.

CHAPTER

2

CONVERSION AND CALL TO THE MINISTRY

Adrian's salvation experience occurred at the age of fourteen while attending a revival crusade held in the Northwood Baptist Church in West Palm Beach, Fla., three blocks from where he lived. About his family's spiritual state prior to that crusade, he says,

> My Dad, I am sure, was a God-fearing man. As a family, we were not anti-God. We were just an average family that was without Christ. As a child, I never heard my father pray. We never had Bible reading in our home, and we did not attend church. I believe my mother was a Christian but had molded her lifestyle to match that of my Dad.

Mr. and Mrs. Frank, neighbors who attended Northwood Church, invited the Rogers family to a crusade where Fred Brown was to be the guest evangelist. One night during that crusade, the evangelist issued a public invitation, asking those who wished to be saved to come forward to receive Christ. Adrian's father stepped forward to give his heart to Christ. Adrian recalls:

> My father's going forward astounded me. I did not know he was thinking about it. To that point everything the preacher had said seemed to pertain to other people.

14

Love Worth Finding

But at the moment my father stepped forward, the message became personal. I was immediately smitten by God's Spirit and knew I needed to do the same thing as my father. When he stepped forward, I did also and made a profession of my faith in Christ.

Reflecting on that night, Adrian says, "I believe an eternal change took place in those moments, and I became a new creature in Christ."

Assurance of Salvation

The two years that followed his conversion experience were marked with spiritual struggle. Adrian describes these years as "being on a spiritual roller coaster, up and down, sincere, but failing in my spiritual life." Cheating in class, fighting at school, bad language, and disobedience continued to be things he battled.

He attributes part of his difficulty to the fact that he was not "well-instructed on how to live the Christian life" following his conversion. "The night I went forward to profess Christ, I was not counseled, nor did they share any Scripture with me. I was not prayed with, nor was I discipled in any way. I left there with all the proclivities of the flesh in me."

Despite the sincerity of his love for Christ, the new convert struggled with a lack of assurance concerning his salvation. The lack of discipleship had created "a sense of spiritual defeatism" within his life. This struggle became so severe that he seriously questioned the authenticity of his salvation experience.

Two years following his public profession of faith in Jesus Christ, Adrian still lacked assurance of his salvation. One night after he had walked me home from church, he stopped at the corner of 39th Street and Calvin Avenue in West Palm Beach. There he prayed for assurance of his salvation. His determination to settle the issue was reinforced by a personal study of the biblical mandate concerning assurance. He recalls, "By this time I had learned that salvation was by grace through faith and that it was possible to have assurance. I had learned those truths, but I still did not know or have assurance."

He says that on that street corner he received full affirmation of his relationship with Christ. Standing there, he looked up into heaven and prayed:

> Lord Jesus, I don't know if I am a true Christian, and the devil is trying to make me doubt it, or if I am still lost and the Holy Spirit is bringing me under conviction. But the one thing I do know is that I am miserable. I need to get some things settled with You for all eternity. I want to know that I am in your kingdom and right with You.
>
> Lord, I do not have assurance, and I do not have comfort, and I need to know that I am saved. From your Word I know that salvation is by grace through faith. So right now with all of my heart, once and for all, now and forever, I trust You only and You always to save me. If I was saved before this, this will not take it away. But if I was not saved, tonight I drive down a peg.
>
> I do not ask for a feeling. I do not look for a sign, for I am willing to stand on your Word. I receive You, Jesus, as my personal Savior and Lord; I commit my life to You.

He recalls that he did not have an ecstasy or a vision that night. "What I did experience were feelings of release, relief, and commitment, and a sense that it was done and I need not look back on it any more. What followed was a wonderful river of God's peace and assurance that began to flow in my heart."

He now reflects on that evening and says, "To this day, I could not absolutely tell you if I truly came to Christ the night I prayed on the street corner or when I went forward as a boy during the crusade. However, that fact makes no difference to me."

Call to the Ministry

Adrian credits Guy Marlowe's ministry at Northwood Baptist Church in West Palm Beach, Fla., as instrumental in helping him respond to God's call into full-time gospel ministry. He says,

> Guy Marlowe was a man who invested his life in the lives of his flock and took an interest in teenagers. Marlowe invited teenagers to participate in ministry when he took them to the Children's Home and out to conduct door-to-door surveys.

Such encouragement left a great impression upon the young Adrian. The pastor became a friend and mentor.

Adrian was an outstanding athlete and captain of the school's championship football team. (He was named to the All-Southern team and received a football scholarship from Stetson University in Deland, Fla. In later years he was inducted into the National Amateur Football Hall of Fame.) Marlowe regularly attended Adrian's football practice sessions and encouraged him to do his best.

As a young man, Adrian had given serious thought to becoming a lawyer or an architect. Yet, Marlowe stressed that God had a plan for everyone's life and that each person should discover God's plan for his or her life. This teaching greatly influenced the young man. He recalls, "I believed God had a plan for my life. It was not a matter of surrendering to do God's will; that was never even an issue. I wanted to know what God's will was for my life. I wasn't running from His will; I wanted to know it."

This struggle was indicative of his determination to please God. As such, Adrian's desire was to discover God's direction for his life.

His call to preach was not a sudden one that came at a single moment in time. Adrian says his call came in stages. During the time Marlowe encouraged him, he prayed, "Lord, what do you want me to do?" Adrian refers to this time in his life as "stage one."

This first stage lasted six months. He then moved into "stage two" with the question, "Lord, do you want me to preach?" He confesses,

> I'm not sure exactly how the germ-thought that God might want me to preach got into my heart. It may have been when I was chosen to be Youth Week pastor and preached my first sermon. After that people began to ask me if I thought God was calling me to preach.
>
> When I was younger attending Sunday School, I was asked by the teacher to lead in prayer. I felt so inadequate that I declined to do so. This embarrassed my teacher and me. I was not afraid of much that moved on the football field, but the thought of public speaking or praying was another matter. I did not think of myself as having any verbal gifts at all.

This predicament weighed heavily on his mind. The call to preach became an increasing burden on his life. Adrian realized the seriousness with which God was calling him to the ministry.

Stages three and four occurred almost simultaneously. Rogers describes stage three as, "Lord, I think You want me to preach," and stage four as, "Lord, if You don't want me to preach, You better let me know!" During these latter stages, Adrian began to pray seriously about preaching the gospel.

Stage five occurred while Adrian attended a retreat at Ridgecrest Baptist Assembly in Ridgecrest, N.C. One night a commitment service was conducted for those who believed God desired them to enter full-time Christian service. He recalls that night:

> Chester Swor was the preacher that evening, but I do not remember what he said. All I remember is that the lady in front of me had a distracting nervous tick in which

her head would jerk at regular intervals that kept me from
paying attention very much. Nevertheless, when the time
came for the commitment service, I went forward and
committed my life to the ministry.

I (his sweetheart, Joyce Gentry) was also attending the retreat and
was standing by his side that evening when Adrian stepped out to publicly
declare that God had called him to preach the gospel. He recalls I squeezed
his hand as we walked out of the meeting that night indicating that I was
pleased with his decision.

The next day, the pastor asked me why I hadn't gone forward—that
God called pastors' wives too. We were too young to be engaged at the
time, but I also felt a call into full-time Christian service.

I was especially interested in Christian education. So I attended a
follow-up meeting the next day and signed a card indicating that I felt
called into Christian service. But I checked the little square that indicated
"undecided" as to exactly what field of Christian service. I can now tell
you that deep within my heart I knew one day I would be Mrs. Adrian
Rogers, pastor's wife.

At the time of his public commitment to enter gospel ministry Adrian
was a junior in high school. He says, "Although I had doubted my salvation,
I have never doubted my call to preach."

He says he occasionally has reflected on what he would have done if
he had not become a preacher, but "I get no satisfactory answers; I have
no desire to do anything but preach." Adrian summarizes his call to the
gospel ministry this way:

> To me, preaching and the ministry is not something I
> "surrendered to." Preaching is something I submitted to
> willingly and gladly. I was thrilled and honored that God
> would call me to preach. I am still amazed that God would
> use me and grateful that He does.

Though God's call came to Adrian Rogers through various means and circumstances, the call was distinct and clear. God's call filled Adrian with the assurance that God desired him to enter the gospel ministry and to preach the Word of God.

CHAPTER

3

EDUCATION

Adrian attended grade school, junior high school, and high school in West Palm Beach, Fla. He considered himself a nominal student. Concerning his academic achievements during his early years of high school, he confesses:

> I was never an academic scholar in high school. God gave me a good mind, and as a result I discovered that I did not have to study to get respectable grades. In my case, that is where a strength became a weakness. I was interested in athletics, and I did not study. In fact, I cannot remember ever bringing a book home from school to study. Either I got it in class, or I did not get it.

Adrian says that during the early part of his schooling he acquired his education through listening, wit, and filibustering in class if he did not know the answer.

Even his call to the gospel ministry his junior year of high school did not improve his poor attitude toward academic study. Football continued to dominate the young student's life.

Near the completion of his junior year of high school, Dean of Students Carl Price confronted Adrian with the prospect of becoming a better student. He challenged Adrian to improve his commitment to academic study. Adrian recounts:

Mr. Price asked me, "Adrian, what do you intend to do when you get out of high school?"

I said, "Mr. Price, God has called me into the ministry, and I want to go to college."

He told me he had examined my school transcript and that my I. Q. and my grades were not commensurate with my ability. Then he asked, "Do you think you can be a minister with the kind of study habits you possess?"

I was deeply convicted, because what he said was true. I said, "Mr. Price, you are right, and I am wrong. I do need to be a better student."

Adrian credits that conversation with changing his attitude concerning academic scholarship. "I appreciated that man caring enough to confront me about my poor study habits. In the providence of God, Mr. Price later moved to Memphis and attended our church. Little did he know, that the high school boy he talked to way back then would one day be the pastor who would perform his funeral."

Price's rebuke of Adrian's poor academic attitude was a turning point in his life. As a result of that conversation, Adrian committed himself to achieving academic excellence.

In 1992 Palm Beach High School selected Adrian and fourteen other former graduates, including Burt Reynolds and George Hamilton, to be inducted into the school's Hall of Fame. Concerning this honor, Adrian says, "I believe my selection was based upon my gospel ministry, and I am grateful for this honor." A small museum was created in West Palm Beach that contains some memorabilia of these honorees.

Leadership Qualities in High School

Young Adrian exhibited leadership qualities even in high school. He was elected president of his senior class and captain of his football team. He and I were chosen as "Most Likely to Succeed" in our senior class.

We led a lunchtime prayer meeting for students in a patio across the street from the school. Even then the students recognized his spiritual leadership.

He was also a leader in his youth group at Northwood Baptist Church, culminating in his choice as Youth Week pastor when he was sixteen. A young couple, Julia Mae and Ryland Mahathey, spent much of their time working with young people in Baptist Training Union and helping young Adrian and me to be leaders in their group.

Another youth worker, Mrs. Lucille Matheson, also saw potential in young Akie and worked with him in memorizing Scripture and encouraging him along the way. Adrian was chosen as a leader of a boys' missionary group called Royal Ambassadors. He coached them in basketball and encouraged them to grow as Christians.

Northwood Baptist Church was not a large church (around 350 in Sunday School attendance), but was filled with loving members who gave much encouragement to their "preacher boy." They provided him with his first opportunities to preach and to enter the young people's "Better Speakers' Tournament."

One faithful member who greatly encouraged young Akie was Slim Holloway, who had been an alcoholic but was now a committed Christian and soul winner. When Adrian got ready to go away to school, Mr. Holloway warned him about liberalism and encouraged him to believe the Bible.

College Years

Upon graduation from Palm Beach High School in 1950, Adrian wanted to attend college and continue his education. His father was not financially able to provide for his son's college education but God provided in various ways. He decided to attend Stetson University in Deland, Fla.

Since I was going to preach, I felt I ought to go to a Baptist school. Stetson had a religion department, and I needed theological training. Also, I wanted to attend the same school as the girl I was dating. So since both of us were Baptist, we thought it would appear normal and natural for both of us to attend our Baptist school. I received a football scholarship and a ministerial scholarship from Stetson, both of which were answers to prayer.

FIRST EXPOSURE TO NEO-ORTHODOXY

When Adrian arrived at Stetson, untrained and open minded, he almost bought into liberal, neo-orthodox theology, which was being espoused in the religion classes he took. But then he began to reflect. He had an open Bible; and he said to himself, "Either what they are teaching is right, and the Bible is wrong; or else what they are teaching is wrong, and the Bible is right." He determined to find the truth for himself and began to study extra-curricular books and materials. One day I said to him, "You had better be careful or you will flunk out of school, because you're taking two courses at one time."

Adrian was grieved, however, at what was being taught in the religion department at Stetson—such as: There is no literal Devil, but he is only the personification of evil. Therefore, demon possession described in the Bible was a form of mental illness.

The inerrancy of Scripture was discarded and many of the miracles in the Bible were discounted. For instance, they taught that Moses did not go through the Red Sea with God holding back the waters, but he waded through the Reed Sea at low tide.

Yet, Adrian's first year at Stetson University provided many opportunities to preach the gospel. He says of those early preaching opportunities:

> Through college days I preached while standing on
> the street corners and bus benches. There were times when
> I would stand in front of the theater and preach as people

exited. My heart's desire was to preach. I also preached in rescue missions and taverns. Those were great days.

On one occasion after preaching on the street, I noticed an attentive man who was nicely dressed. I approached him and asked him if he were a Christian.

He replied in the affirmative and then began to ask me about myself. I told him that I was a student at Stetson University, but was not doing this under the auspices of the school. They might not even approve if they knew about it.

In subsequent days we became good friends. He was a successful businessman and encouraged me in the ministry. When his church at Merritt Island, Fla., was without a pastor, he recommended me to the church. My ministry there was wonderful and fruitful.

I learned a lesson in life. There was a connection between preaching on the street corner and being the pastor of a dynamic and growing church. He that is faithful in that which is least, is faithful also in that which is much.

Through his zeal for preaching the gospel, Adrian soon acquired some notoriety as a preacher. Churches began to invite him to preach revival meetings and youth crusades. He considered a life as an evangelist, but instead he found himself being an evangelistic pastor of growing churches.

In his second year at Stetson Adrian met Joe Boatwright in the trailer park where they were living. The following week Adrian couldn't put up with what the chapel speaker was teaching, so he got up to leave. Joe was coming around the corner, having had the same thought. They began to discuss some of the liberal teachings they had encountered at Stetson.

At that moment a lifelong friendship began between Joe and Adrian. Since Joe's wife is also Joyce, we would soon become known as Joyce "B" and Joyce "R."

CHAPTER

4

KEY EVENTS

During the four years of study at Stetson University, three key events occurred which significantly influenced his life. The first event was our engagement and marriage. Joyce Louise Gentry became Mrs. Adrian Rogers. Adrian and I became engaged on Christmas Eve during our freshman year of college. We had picked out an engagement ring earlier that year. Adrian put it on layaway and made monthly payments until it was paid for. It wasn't a large diamond, but I treasured it.

Years later when Adrian offered to buy me a larger diamond, I refused because of sentimental reasons. However, many years later I lost the diamond out of my ring, and Adrian then bought me another.

I took the remainder of my engagement ring and the narrow gold wedding band and had them fashioned into another ring (still a sentimental treasure) that I wear on my right hand.

We were married on September 2, 1951, at our home church, Northwood Baptist in West Palm Beach. We were excited to begin our new life together. My parents continued to send me to college, where I completed my major in religion.

"Lengthen Your Cords And Strengthen Your Stakes."

After our first year of marriage we purchased a twenty-five foot house trailer with no inside bathroom facilities. There was a bathhouse and laundry room near our trailer. We loved living in our little trailer-home and eventually added a "spare room" covered with an awning.

One night during a driving rain, Adrian heard a noise. We went outside to see the screened walls of the patio bending toward the middle and the canvas awning filling with water. When we pushed the awning up in one place, the water just moved to another. Pressing on the awning caused it to leak, so we both had water dripping from our elbows.

The awning was anchored by ropes tied to stakes in the ground. But clearly the stakes were too weak and the cords were too short. For we found that all of the stakes had pulled out of the wet soil. Adrian has used this as an illustration while preaching on the topic of "Lengthening Your Cords and Strengthening Your Stakes." He has endeavored to drive the stakes of God's Word deep into the ministry God has given him. This is the reason he can lengthen his cords and enlarge the place of his ministry.

Called to His First Church

The second key event transpired during his freshman year when the First Baptist Church of Fellsmere, Fla., asked Adrian to be their pastor. It was the first (and only) Baptist church in a town of about five hundred people. The church was made up of a small number of loving people. Characterizing his first pastorate, Adrian reflects, "I was nineteen years of age and utterly untrained. I am sure my preaching was greatly lacking in form and content, but God graciously and visibly worked. There were commitments of repentance and tears of joy from the start in that little congregation."

Adrian's ordination to the gospel ministry occurred on May 8, 1951, commensurate with the young pastor's call to the Fellsmere church. After being called to the church, Adrian relinquished his football scholarship to allow him a greater opportunity to be a loving husband to me and a faithful pastor to the church.

The Fellsmere church was rustic, to say the least. The building had an unpainted concrete floor, unpainted cement block walls, and no ceiling. Rafters cut from rough lumber were overhead. The building was lighted with bare bulbs dangling by their cords from the ceiling. The pews were not pews at all, but two two-by-eight boards connected by an iron bracket—one to sit on and one to lean back on. There was no running water, no baptistery, and no water fountain. Those who needed a restroom walked across the street to a neighbor's house.

It wasn't the Taj Mahal, but it was beautiful to us. It was the scene of a great revival spirit. The church almost doubled in one year with fifty-one baptisms.

Adrian bought a 1936 Plymouth sedan for $150.00. It took us from Deland (where the university was) to Fellsmere, an almost 300-mile round trip each weekend. The salary was $25 a week with no car allowance. Later the salary was increased to $30. Somehow, we felt it was too much and gave half of the increase back to the church. God provided for all of our needs.

Those were days of heaven on earth. No church had a sweeter fellowship. Each week the untrained pastor had to dig and scratch for two fresh sermons. Yet no spiritually sensitive person would deny that God was at work.

We had three primary places to lay our heads on a Saturday night. One was Mrs. Shearer's boarding house. It was old and ram shackled, but it was a place to sleep and provided lavish home-cooked meals.

On other occasions we would spend the night with Lloyd and Mattie Ingram, who operated a small mercantile store and were leaders in the church. There were four churches in the small town of Fellsmere. When the Ingrams arrived in Fellsmere, they were invited to attend another church by a member because "the best people" went there. Mr. Ingram replied, "Not any more."

The Ingrams were gracious to us, and many times would have us over for Sunday dinner. They would almost always have a delicious roast with vegetables, which was a treat.

The third place we would sometimes spend the weekend was with Neil and Frankie Shearer. Neil was an unlettered man who made his living as a frogger and had a great heart for God. On one occasion they served us frog legs and gator tail.

THE PASTOR'S FIRST BAPTISM

Adrian performed his first baptism in a canal, just outside of Fellsmere. The person to be baptized was a young woman named Willie Mae Vereen, whom Adrian had led to Christ.

The church family gathered at the banks and sang a hymn. Adrian then had a frightening thought. He had never baptized anyone, and no one had instructed him on how to do it. How should he stand? Where would he take hold of the candidate? Should she bend her knees or lay over backwards in the water?

These and other questions caused a little concern in the young pastor's mind. Nonetheless, it was time for the baptism. The banks of the canal were somewhat steep and slippery, but he made his way down and stood in the water about waist deep. Then other men helped Willie Mae down to the water.

It was a chilly day in Florida, and Adrian remembers Willie Mae sucking in her breath through clenched teeth with sort of a hissing sound as she touched the water. All went well with no major problems. Somehow, Adrian managed to get her under water, "buried in his likeness," and then up again, "raised to walk in the newness of life" (Rom. 6:4; NKJV). The church members went on their way rejoicing. What pastor can ever forget his first baptism? It was a poignant moment.

We'll always remember those wonderful church members. They loved us and treated us as members of their own family.

I'll never forget people like "Granny" McMillan. We ate many a home-cooked meal at her table. In my mind I can still hear her singing alto to "God Is Calling the Prodigal."

This initial ministry lasted until Adrian graduated from Stetson University. God greatly blessed those three years, and the lives of many people were transformed.

JOYCE AND ME AND BABY MAKES THREE

In our junior year of college we decided to start a family. We reasoned that I had finished my major in Bible and would attend a year of seminary. There were two disappointing miscarriages and a threatened miscarriage.

But the day Adrian walked across the platform to receive his B.A., I was seated in the audience, proudly holding my B.A. —our three-month-old B-A-B-Y, Stephen Michael Rogers. Now it was "Joyce and me and baby makes three." Steve had been born on February 26, 1954.

Farewell to Fellsmere

After a grand and glorious day when every seat in the auditorium was filled, we said goodbye to our beloved church at Fellsmere. It was a sad, but fond, farewell as the tears began to flow.

By this time the church had running water, restrooms and a baptistry. The rustic benches had been replaced with theater seats. The ceiling was ceiled with beautiful ponderosa pine, and adequate lighting was installed. A new educational wing was also added, and the pastor now had a small office. But greater than these material blessings were the lives that were transformed.

A half century later we still hear from those children who came to faith in Christ under our ministry. Years later, Buddy Johns became the pastor of the Fellsmere church. He had been a ten-year-old boy when Adrian was the pastor.

We went back for the church's fiftieth anniversary. There were few adults living who had been members when we were there. One was Neal Shearer, who was now eighty years old. What a nostalgic day that was!

The church pianist, who had been three years old when we left Fellsmere, was now fifty years old. Our son Steve, who was a three-month-old baby when we left, attended the memorable celebration with us.

CHAPTER

5

SEMINARY DAYS AND
WAVELAND BAPTIST CHAPEL

Adrian spent the summer between college and seminary in fruitful preaching engagements. Sometimes Steve and I would stay with my parents, and sometimes we would go along to his meetings.

After much prayerful consideration, we had chosen the New Orleans Baptist Theological Seminary in New Orleans, La., as the place to continue his education. Adrian recalls how we made that choice:

> One, I liked where the seminary was located. The school was in the southeastern region of the United States, and I thought I knew more about the characteristics of the area. Two, New Orleans was an area that needed preachers and needed the gospel. I wanted to go somewhere where I could reach people for Christ, and New Orleans seemed more like a mission field to me.

Such conditions supported his dual compulsion to preach the gospel and to receive an education. He was convinced that the seminary in New Orleans could provide him with an opportunity to fulfill both objectives.

For our first two weeks in New Orleans we stayed with friends we had met in college, Bob and Barbara Barwick. The Barwicks let us sleep on their mattress, and they slept on the box springs. There was no living room furniture, but they did have a television. Sitting on the floor, leaning against the wall, we spent happy evenings watching television and having wonderful fellowship.

There was a six-month waiting period for married student housing on the seminary campus. After two weeks, an apartment in the Florida Avenue Housing Project came available. One hundred other seminary families lived there also. We moved into a third-floor apartment. The rent and utilities came to eighteen dollars a month, because we paid according to our income.

Adrian had gotten a job with the local pest control company for a dollar an hour. He called to make appointments for free termite inspections. He spent much time with a flashlight crawling under houses. He made twenty dollars a week, and we lived off the five hundred dollars in our savings account for the remainder of our expenses.

Called to Waveland Baptist Chapel

After six months the money was running out, but just that week a friend called and asked if Adrian wanted to preach at the Waveland Baptist Chapel in Waveland, Miss., sixty miles from the seminary. Indeed, he did! We made the trip to Waveland, and he preached.

That evening after the service they asked us to wait in the car while they voted to call Adrian as pastor of the little church. We were grateful, because we wanted a church so much. God also provided for us financially, for the money in our savings account had just run out that week.

There were only twenty-five church members and fewer in attendance. We moved on to the "church field," and Adrian commuted to school Tuesday through Friday of every week. Then he became the pastor to this little church on the long weekends. It was a difficult time, but there were also new friends and many wonderful experiences.

"THERE'S NO PLACE LIKE HOME"

Two houses where we lived while in Waveland were especially

memorable. One place we called the captain's house because an old retired sea captain owned it. It was located not far from the water on the Gulf Coast. He and his wife lived upstairs, and we lived on the lower floor.

The first house on this property had been destroyed by a fierce hurricane. The Captain built another house much farther back from the water. Cement was poured about four feet up into the walls on the bottom floor for security. The Captain loved Irish ballads, and we woke every morning to songs like "O Danny Boy."

Steve was around two years old when we moved to Waveland. Adrian was gone from 7 a.m to 7 p.m. every day Tuesday through Friday, so Steve and I spent a lot of time together.

I read books and sang songs and Bible choruses to him. We bought him a little record player, and he played his few records over and over. We took long walks along the Gulf shore in front of our house, and we would sing these songs. He could sing twenty little songs by heart when he was just two years old.

It was while we lived at the Captain's house that his sister, Gayle, was born. By then Steve was twenty-eight months old. The house was in an area that had only one way out, and it was the road beside the Gulf of Mexico. Two weeks from the baby's due date there were hurricane warnings. We remembered how the Captain's first house had been destroyed during a hurricane.

Not wanting to alarm me, Adrian calmly told me that he and the Captain thought it would be wise if we stayed with friends just three miles away—closer to the hospital, but not near the water just in case I might deliver early.

Adrian did not tell me until later that waves were coming over the vehicles traveling along the Gulf road.

We arrived safely at our friends' house, and all was well. The baby was not born until two days after the hurricane on June 16, 1956. It was a girl, and we named her Gayle Christine. So our little family grew to four, and Steve and Gayle became great friends.

THE MATHIS HOUSE

The other house that especially stood out in our minds was the Mathis house. Mr. Mathis had been the one and only church pianist. He and his wife moved out of town and let us rent their house. Adrian told me that I should learn how to play the piano even if it were only three songs. So, he bought me a used piano. As soon as I had learned to play three songs, I began to play for the church services. The songs? "There Is A Fountain," "What A Friend We Have in Jesus," and "Where He Leads Me."

One evening at the Mathis house when Adrian was gone, I heard a noise under the house, which was built up off of the ground. It frightened me and I called Adrian on the phone to ask him to come home from a meeting he was attending.

We couldn't figure out what the noise was until the next morning when Adrian looked under the house and saw a mama sow and her little piglets. The mama sow was rubbing her back on the floor joist, making the mysterious noise.

He ran the pigs out from under the house, but that is not the end of the story. All that Mrs. Pig and her offspring did was to move a little farther from the house and make a mud hole for her new apartment. It didn't help the appearance of the yard. When Adrian yelled at the pigs or threw rocks at them, they would move a little and then come back.

Adrian decided, "This is war!" He went to a fireworks store and bought some cherry bombs. He thought, "This will do it." So he tossed the cherry bombs near the pig, but all they did was result in a disdainful look.

Adrian then believed it was time to bring in the "heavy artillery." So he wrapped the fuses of three cherry bombs together. When he lit and threw them, that did it! The war was over. Adrian watched as the mother pig and her piglets moved in retreat down the country road to be seen no more.

I also recall how cold it was the last winter we lived in that house. There was just a single floor and sometimes the cold air would come through the cracks. My feet stayed cold all winter long.

A Second Baby Boy

This house was also memorable because we were living here when our third baby, Philip Gentry, was born on February 26, 1958—on his brother Steve's fourth birthday. What a wonderful family God had given us.

Yet, life was lonely at times for me. We only had one car, so I stayed home with the children when Adrian was gone to school. The year I had planned to attend seminary gradually slipped by with the birth of two babies. I was always a student, though, and ordered Bible courses from the "Back to the Bible" radio broadcast. I would listen to the program and do the homework I had ordered. I learned much listening to Theodore Epp, the outstanding Bible teacher on this helpful program.

I loved being a pastor's wife, homemaker and a mother, so it was all worth the sacrifice. I gave my love especially to the teenagers in the church. I enjoyed teaching them and having them come to our home. There were two teenage boys whom Steve called "his boys."

Waveland was a difficult place in which to minister. It was predominately Roman Catholic, which made it hard to establish an evangelical church. Yet there were still some who received Christ and as a result were dramatically changed.

Waveland was a weekend retreat community for many who lived in New Orleans. It seemed that their major passion was fishing, boiling crabs, and drinking Jax beer. They did not come to Waveland to go to church.

One snowy Sunday few turned out to church. In fact, there were only eight in attendance and our little family made up four of the eight. Adrian, normally optimistic, considered dropping out of seminary and moving to a more productive church field so he could see more fruit for his ministry. A large and fast growing church in South Carolina had contacted him. The pastor in that church was not able to keep up with the growth and the church was looking for new leadership.

On that snowy day with only a handful present, he began to think about the opportunity and challenge of this other church.

But that feeling stayed no longer than a week, and he was happily back to the task at Waveland. The work was hard but fruitful. The church building was a wooden barrack. All of the classes met in the small building, separated only by curtains. Adrian felt educational space and a nursery were needed. There were those in the small church who could not see his vision nor share his enthusiasm.

However, Adrian was able to get some plans from the Church Architecture Division of the Southern Baptist Convention. The church had no building fund. With help from the Home Mission Board there was just enough money to meet weekly expenses.

Yet the young pastor wanted the building built. Not knowing where the resources would come from, he got two young men and three shovels; and the three of them began to dig a footing for the foundation. One lady, whose husband was in the building business, saw what was happening and came to the three young men working in the blazing sun. She said, "You will never build this building. The young preacher knew then in his heart that it would be built, and praise God, it was!

The church grew under Rogers leadership from twenty-five to around seventy-five members. Although some said it could never be done, a new educational building was built, and for the first time a small nursery was included.

When Steve was small there was not a church nursery. I would usually sit on the back row and let Steve sit in the windowsill and lean against the screen. One Sunday as Adrian was preaching, he heard a big commotion, and when he looked up I was running out of the church. It was then he realized Steve had fallen out of the window. He fortunately fell on a bush and was not hurt. We have laughed about that incident many times.

Graduation from Seminary

In January 1958, Adrian graduated from the New Orleans Baptist Theological Seminary with a Bachelor of Divinity degree. The seminary later reissued the degree as a Master of Theology. Although he considered doing doctoral work, he never enrolled for further theological training. However, he was committed to be a continuing student.

Six Honorary Degrees Conferred

Six honorary degrees have been conferred on Adrian since seminary. The first, granted in 1972, was a Doctor of Divinity degree from Trinity College, Dunedin, Fla. The second, awarded in 1979, was a Doctor of Litterarum from California Graduate School of Theology, Glendale, Calif. The third degree, awarded in 1984, was a Doctor of Divinity from Toccoa Falls (Ga.) College. The fourth, awarded in 1985, was a Doctor of Sacred Theology degree from Southwest Baptist University, Bolivar, Mo. The fifth, a Doctor of Divinity degree from Hannibal (Mo.) LaGrange College, was granted in 1985. The sixth, awarded in 2003, was a Doctor of Divinity, from Liberty University, Lynchburg, Va.

Adrian says the focuses of his studies since graduating from the seminary have been related to the areas of preaching and to the Word of God. However, his preaching was well rounded in many areas. He has a special interest in prophecy, the Spirit-filled life, and the types of Christ in the Bible.

Resigned from Waveland Baptist Chapel

When Adrian was getting ready to graduate from seminary, he was praying about his future. He spoke of being on a three-legged stool. He was seriously considering missions, evangelism, and the pastorate.

During this time two letters arrived simultaneously in his post office box, both from relatively small churches in Florida. Each had an average Sunday School attendance of 100. Both said they felt it was God's will for Adrian to be their pastor. Adrian knew one of them (or possibly both) had to be wrong. After prayer he wrote both churches and respectfully declined.

The Fort Pierce church, however, responded, "Please reconsider." From an outward appearance the church was not an attractive prospect. A succession of pastors had each stayed two years or less. The property was limited, and the growth was stagnant.

After prayer Adrian and I felt we should go to the Park View Baptist Church. Despite the challenges, we felt the inner nudge of the Spirit and decided to say yes to Park View.

Before answering, though, Adrian told his little fellowship at his seminary church in Waveland that he would be moving to Florida to pastor this church. He spoke to the people at Waveland of how God had impressed his heart and then to make it more dramatic he said, "A nail-pierced hand has pointed to Florida, and I must follow." He thought, *Who could argue with a nail-pierced hand?*

Of course, Adrian and I shed tears, but we submitted to the will of God.

Yet Adrian had not given a formal acceptance to the Fort Pierce church. Upon arriving home that Sunday, we heard the phone ringing. On the phone was a Mr. Graham who was with the pulpit committee of the First Baptist Church of one of Florida's three largest cities. This committee was interested in speaking to Adrian about being the senior pastor. Mr. Graham began to regale him with facts about the church. He spoke of a salary (more than twice that of Fort Pierce). He spoke of the support staff that served the church. It seemed to be everything that the Fort Pierce church was not. It was what many would call "a great opportunity."

At first Adrian was interested, but in the middle of the conversation he was smitten by the Holy Spirit: "Did you not tell those people this morning that a nail-pierced hand was pointing you to Fort Pierce? Why are you so fickle?"

Adrian then knew this was a test of his honesty and faithfulness to his word. He recalls, "It seemed that God had written across the dining room wall stretched from floor to ceiling, "This is a test." So, in the middle of the conversation with Mr. Graham he said, "I am sorry, sir, but I cannot talk to you anymore. I am already committed to Fort Pierce, and that is what I will do. Thank you and goodbye."

So, we said another sad farewell, this time to Waveland members who had become well-loved friends whom we would remember forever.

CHAPTER

6

A NEW BEGINNING AT PARK VIEW BAPTIST CHURCH

It was while at Park View that our little Philip stepped into heaven. One of the results was a deepening work of the Holy Spirit in our lives. But our time there was not all sorrow.

The church had an attendance of one hundred in Sunday School when Adrian went to Park View. Six years later when we left, the attendance had grown to 650.

When we moved to Fort Pierce, we lived in the pastorium, next door to the church. This was convenient, but also easy for people to just drop in. The first Sunday morning a family who always arrived early came to the back door. It wasn't locked, so the man walked in without knocking. We never left the doors unlocked again. And although we were grateful for the provisions that had been made for us, we were glad when the church nursery outgrew its facilities in the first six months. As a result the church turned the pastorium into an enlarged nursery building and bought a new pastorium about a mile from the church.

GOING DEEPER INTO JESUS

Although when Adrian was a young man he experienced a total surrender of his life to Christ with a desire to be used by God, the experience of losing Philip to SIDS took him deeper into longing to know Jesus and to be like Him.

Around this time while in a Christian bookstore, Adrian casually picked up *The Saving Life of Christ* by Major Ian Thomas. This turned out to be a God-ordained circumstance. The book's message, at the same time simple and profound, was that Jesus is the one person who has ever lived the Christian life. The life we live is not ours, but Jesus living His life through us.

He has never asked us to do anything for Him but is always willing to do something with us and through us. This truth may sound simplistic perhaps, even a play on words, but it goes to the core of the Christian life. We discovered that Christ within us was sufficient to meet every challenge we face and that He is always sufficient to give comfort as we walk through the valley of sorrow.

Fruitful Years at Park View

The years at the Park View Baptist Church left an indelible mark on us. It was there that Adrian honed the preaching skills that would continue to mold his ministry in years to come.

It was then that he began "Daybreak," an early morning radio broadcast that was done mostly live, beginning at 6:45 a.m.

One morning we both overslept. We awoke at 6:42 a.m. In desperation Adrian called the station and asked them to "patch him in" on the telephone. He then asked me to bring him a Bible, and in his nightwear and down upon one knee by a table he began to preach. He doesn't remember much of what he said that day, and he imagines that those who listened did not remember it as a monumental message. But we sure remember the hilarity of the scene.

Our biggest memory of that episode is of my trying to hold back laughter and how ridiculous he looked coming from a hard sleep, down on his knee with a Bible in one hand and the telephone in the other. He had often told other preachers, "If you're asked to preach, and someone would drop a handkerchief, you ought to be on the second point before it hits the ground." In that instance he learned to practice what he preached.

Another Defining Moment

Another defining moment in Adrian's ministry occurred at the Baptist State Convention held in Jacksonville, Fla. Adrian loved his school, Stetson University and had made many wonderful friends there.

When he returned to Florida after graduating from seminary, he discovered that the liberal, neo-orthodox teaching had gotten worse at Stetson and moral standards had dropped. As a result of his grieved spirit over these things, he offered a motion at the Florida State Baptist Convention that support for the University be dropped from the budget. He did this with "fear and trembling," because this was his alma mater.

There were repercussions to his action. A vice-president of the school wrote a letter to Adrian in which he described a "high road" and a "low road." He said, "I have seen many take the 'high road' and have a fruitful ministry and others take the 'low road' and how sad and untimely was their end."

Despite that warning and veiled threat, God continued to bless Adrian's ministry and his concerns seemed to be prophetic. Although his original motion failed, the school continued to drift toward the left. Many years later it was removed from the convention's budget for these reasons.

Interestingly, while Adrian has been elected three times as president of the Southern Baptist Convention and has been cited as an outstanding alumnus of the New Orleans Baptist Theological Seminary, he has never been recognized by his college alma mater. Nevertheless, he has no regrets.

I've always been so proud to be married to a man of courage and conviction. What people might think never bothered me; I supported Adrian for taking a bold stand for the inerrancy of the Word of God and against worldliness.

The Desire of Our Hearts

While we were at Park View, God blessed us with two other children sixteen months apart, David (July 30, 1960) and Janice (December 4, 1961). Although both pregnancies were in danger of miscarriage, both babies were born healthy. We had always wanted four children, and God gave us the desire of our hearts. But fulfilling that desire meant there were two babies in diapers at one time. Life was busy, but there were lots of wonderful times with these delightful children. They grew up to become great friends, and Steve and Gayle loved their younger brother and sister.

THE CHURCH GREW AND PROSPERED

Park View Church grew in numbers and faith. It increased in size more than six times the original number in six years. The Sunday School grew from 100 to 650 in attendance.

Adrian added an assistant pastor/music minister, Jeff Stiles. Stiles later became a pastor himself, but he and his wife, Louise, have remained our lifelong friends.

During our years of service there, the lives of many people were changed for eternity. These were precious years with precious people.

CHAPTER

7

FIRST BAPTIST CHURCH, MERRITT ISLAND, FLA.

It was a bittersweet time when we said goodbye to the saints at Fort Pierce and answered a call to the First Baptist Church of Merritt Island, Fla. Merritt Island was contiguous to the Kennedy Space Center. Many of the engineers and technical people who would put the first man on the moon, attended the church. The church's motto became, "Pointing men beyond the stars."

The area was booming with new, young families. The median age was twenty-seven. The growth of the church was dramatic with Sunday School attendance increasing from the 300s to 2000. This put an enormous strain on the facilities of the church at the time.

It became evident that more buildings were needed. The church began a massive building program to try to stay ahead of the growth. The pastor and the membership knew that God was doing something unique.

Minister of Music James Whitmire, called it "the days of Camelot." Souls were saved in almost every service, causing the church to lead the Florida Baptist Convention in baptisms almost every year during Adrian's eight-year ministry there.

The Merritt Island church had to make adjustments to manage the crowd and to reach more people for Christ. Besides the new building, we added new staff and the ministry became more complicated. Thomas Clayton came as the first minister of education and became a great help in these years of growth.

Because of the pressures of management and ministry, Adrian found himself in conflict between family life and church life. For a period of time we wrestled with these problems. Adrian came to realize that while he loved the church, his first priority was God, his second was his family and next was the church. In reality, he came to see that the church was Jesus' bride—not his. He also learned a wonderful truth—that the more he modeled these priorities, the clearer became the silent sermon that spoke to other families in the church.

Adrian perceived that the First Baptist Church of Merritt Island was his lifelong ministry, but nonetheless, the "days of Camelot" would come to an end. He was featured in the Sunday Supplement of the Brevard County newspaper. In an interview for the article, Adrian was asked how long he would be at Merritt Island. His answer was, "I expect to go to heaven from Merritt Island." But that was not to be.

CHAPTER

8

THE CALL TO HISTORIC BELLEVUE BAPTIST CHURCH

The historic Bellevue Baptist Church of Memphis, Tenn., made famous by the great preacher Robert G. Lee, was in need of a pastor. When we were juniors in high school, Dr. Lee came to the First Baptist Church of West Palm Beach. We went to hear the then-well-known preacher preach his famous sermon, "Pay Day Some Day." We couldn't even dream, at that moment, one day we would be pastor and wife of the church where Dr. Lee was then the pastor.

Bellevue grew enormously under Dr. Lee's thirty-three-year leadership. He was succeeded by Ramsey Pollard, who also was well known for his leadership skills across the Southern Baptist Convention. Pollard served the church for twelve years.

THE PULPIT COMMITTEE'S SEARCH

A pulpit committee was formed to seek out a new pastor. The name *Adrian Rogers* came to them from several individuals. The committee attended the Southern Baptist Pastors' Conference to listen to the preachers who were on the program. Adrian was one of the featured preachers. The title of his message was, "The Making of a Man of God." He had no idea that the pulpit committee from Bellevue Baptist Church was present, but the message could not have been more pertinent.

After the conference some of the committee spoke to a pastor friend who knew Adrian. They asked about his character, his church, his convictions and his leadership abilities. This friend knew Adrian was identified by his strict standards concerning the Word of God and personal holiness in the life of the church.

Later at the convention this friend saw Adrian and told him of his visit with the pulpit committee and his report on Adrian's strict convictions. They had a good-natured laugh over the whole matter, because he had absolutely no inclination to leave Merritt Island. The affair seemed so inconsequential that he failed to mention it to me for several weeks.

One evening as we were returning home from a walk, Adrian recalled the incident and asked, "Guess what, Joyce? When I preached in Philadelphia, a pulpit committee from Bellevue Baptist Church was there." He then told me what the mutual friend had told the committee about his standards and convictions. At this we both had a good-natured laugh, and I spoke some prophetic words: "If they spoke to you now, you'd have to know that God was in it."

Adrian replied with a smile, "That's for sure." Little did he know the import of his words.

A Vacation Providentially Interrupted

We left for a vacation with three of our children in a motor home to visit the northeastern United States. Steve stayed at home. Adrian called home from somewhere in Georgia, and Steve reported that a member of the Bellevue pulpit committee had called. The committee member asked Steve to relay the message to his Dad that they would like him to return the call as soon as possible.

Adrian took the number but had no inclination to call. I told him, "Out of sheer courtesy, you should at least return the call."

Adrian went into a phone booth at a campground in Lynchburg, Va., and spoke to Roland Maddox, who asked if it were possible for some of the members from the pulpit committee to fly where he was and talk.

Adrian was polite but said, "I'm honored that you would be interested, but I've absolutely no inclination to leave my present pastorate.

Maddox persisted however and told Adrian of the investment they had made visiting Philadelphia and Merritt Island and gathering background material. He said, "The least you can do is talk with us."

Adrian had no desire for the committee to fly to where he was, thereby making him more indebted emotionally to these people.

He then had an idea. He said, "I'll tell you what I'll do. I am in a motor home with no fixed itinerary. I will drive over there and have a talk with you." We did not realize at that time how far it was from Lynchburg to Memphis.

Originally, we made the trip more out of courtesy than anything else. But in the ensuing days as Adrian talked and prayed with the committee, he began to get a strange feeling in his heart, "Could this be the will of God for me?" He knew he had no right to his own life and must open his heart to hear God's direction.

The committee began to share about the kind of pastor they wanted. The spirit of God was present and on several occasions tears would flow from the eyes of some committee members. Adrian and I began to ponder these things in our hearts. The committee was unanimous in their intent and asked if they could present Adrian as a candidate for pastor to the Bellevue church.

He was not willing to go that far. In a spirit of compromise, he said he would pray about the possibility of going to Bellevue to preach, but not as a candidate for the pulpit.

He wanted to see if there was any "spiritual connection" with the people.

"I'd Be a Fool to Leave Here."

The Rogers family returned home to Merritt Island. We fasted and prayed about whether or not Adrian should go and preach at Bellevue. While all of these thoughts were being pondered in his mind, he attended the Sunday evening services at Merritt Island.

The youth choir had just returned from a summer choir tour and was singing a home concert.

The church building was filled with great music, joyful hearts, and happy faces. The presence of God was so evident. After the service, we made our way to the car. It was a beautiful summer night in Florida. The moon was shining brightly. There was a gentle breeze in the palm trees, and fragrance of gardenias was in the air. The whole evening seemed to be perfect, and Adrian said to me, "I'd be a fool to leave here." But the matter of Bellevue still "hung heavily over us" and needed to be decided.

We began to discuss the possibility of going to Bellevue on a scale from one to ten. Adrian hardly got above five, but in my heart I often felt like it was a ten.

He then decided that he should at least go to Memphis and preach at Bellevue Church. He told his deacons at Merritt Island where he was going and what had been going on in his heart and life; but that he had no desire to leave Merritt Island. Little did he expect what was about to transpire.

We spent a time of intense prayer with the pulpit committee before the coming Sunday. Somehow, however, Adrian and the pulpit committee got "their wires crossed." He thought that he was only filling the pulpit for a Sunday. Yet before that historic Sunday had ended, he had accepted the call to Bellevue.

A Unanimous Call to Bellevue

Adrian describes what transpired on that awesome day, "From the opening note of the morning music there was an obvious visitation of the Holy Spirit. This was not imaginary but was experienced by everyone present that day."

Adrian preached with power a sermon titled, "Faith and How to Have It." He felt an unusual freedom in preaching that day. The air seemed to be filled with "spiritual electricity."

At the close of the service we were asked if we would retire to the pastor's study so the pulpit committee could bring a report. He did not know that he was being presented to the church for a vote upon him as the new pastor.

They brought us from the pastor's study and announced the vote concerning him was unanimous. Adrian was stunned! He asked the presiding chairman, Gene Howard, and the pulpit committee, "Are you asking me to be your pastor?" The answer was a resounding, "Yes!" That was a defining moment. We would ordinarily discuss and pray about matters like this until we came to unanimity. But there was Adrian on the platform, in front of the entire congregation. In reflecting on that moment he remembers hearing himself saying, "Very well, I accept!"

It was for him a strange thing—a "God thing." There was the deeply moving service that morning and then the misunderstanding between him and the committee. In Adrian's mind he was not being presented as a candidate for Bellevue's pastor. He was deeply moved by what had transpired in this chain of events.

After shaking some hands, Adrian asked to be alone. He went to the pastor's study. The whole episode was beginning to sink in. He remembers lying face down on the carpet and weeping. He prayed, "Oh God, what have I done? What is happening here? What will those dear people at Merritt Island think? He felt almost like a man who had left his wife for another. But it was done, and there was no turning back.

I later told him that God had been confirming the decision in my heart and I believed it would be God's will. Therefore my heart was at rest when Adrian accepted the call to Bellevue.

Goodbye to the Wonderful Merritt Island Church

Right after the morning service, a Bellevue member had called Merritt Island to tell a deacon there, "Well, you just lost your pastor." Then there was the journey home to face the sad farewells. That part wasn't easy. Saying goodbye to precious friends and staff members was like tearing away a part of our very lives.

This was an interruption in many lives—not the least being our children. Steve had just been home from Bible school in England for a couple of months. He was to start college in the fall. The hardest thing about the move to Memphis was leaving Steve in Florida. We made plans for him to stay with Adrian's parents and to attend Palm Beach Atlantic College. I remember praying, "Oh God, please let our son have a love for Bellevue and feel like it is home."

It took time, but eventually that prayer was answered.

Gayle, who was sixteen at the time, wanted to remain at Merritt Island with friends through football season. (The team was projected to win the championship.) So she moved to Memphis in time for Thanksgiving. Gayle wasn't opposed to the move. In fact, after the visit to Memphis on our vacation, the first thing she did when she got home was to pack a big box of her books. In her heart she knew this was God's will, but it was still hard.

That meant our two youngest children, David and Janice, eleven and ten years old at the time, were the only ones to make the original move. There was a bridge that spanned the Indian River from Merritt Island to Cocoa, Fla., where we would meet U.S. Highway 1 for the journey to Memphis, Tenn. As we reached half way over the bridge, all of us broke down and cried. This represented a huge part of our lives, and it was a final farewell.

Oh God, help us on this new journey of faith.

CHAPTER

9

A NEW BEGINNING
AT BELLEVUE

The majority of the congregation at Merritt Island had been young married adults. Now Adrian looked out over a congregation filled with gray hair. How would they respond to a pastor who was just forty years old? It had been twelve years since a Bellevue pastor had been under fifty-seven years old and many years since there had been school-aged children in the pastor's home. But God's Holy Spirit joined the young pastor and wife to these people, and there was a bond of love from the beginning. I remember telling Adrian, "The older ladies pat me on the arm when I walk down the halls and tell me that they love me. How can they love me? They don't even know me." Yet they did love me. They loved me by faith, and I loved them back. It has been a mutual spiritual love affair ever since.

Changes in the Rogers' Family

Soon Bellevue and Memphis became home, and the children made friends and settled into the children's and youth activities. Gayle became a great helper and friend to the youth director, Dotie Morgan. The children participated in sports and music programs, retreats and Bible studies.

When David and Janice became teenagers, Dan Carter was the youth minister. He had a heart for missions, and our younger children became involved in youth mission trips to the Navajo Indians in Arizona. They also were a part of the youth choir under the leadership of Jim Whitmire, who had joined the Bellevue staff as youth minister of music. They loved choir tours and being a part of the singing Christmas tree, which became a beloved Bellevue tradition.

STEVE AND HIS BRIDE CINDI

Then wedding bells began to chime in the Rogers' household. Steve was the first to get married. He married his high school sweetheart, Cindi Bradley, from Merritt Island. The family ventured back to Florida for this happy occasion. The ladies of Bellevue gave a church-wide wedding shower for the young couple, who came to visit for the weekend. The love of the Bellevue ladies made Cindi and Steve feel like they were part of the Bellevue family.

Steve and Cindi moved to Memphis where Steve completed his degree in business and music. They then moved back to Florida and a beautiful blonde baby girl was born—Adrienne Renae. We missed them so much, but appreciated opportunities for them to visit Memphis and for us to visit Florida. Renae is now grown and is a lovely young woman who is a gifted graphic artist and designer of girls' hats and sports equipment.

GAYLE AND HER GROOM MIKE

Wedding bells chimed again—this time for Gayle and Mike Foster. Gayle had met Mike while she was working on the secretarial staff at Bellevue. He was attending Mid America Baptist Theological Seminary and was working as a "work-shipper" on the Bellevue staff.

They were married in the Bellevue sanctuary at 70 N. Bellevue Avenue. Mike was ordained to the ministry and after their honeymoon, they moved to Euless, Texas, where Mike became the minister of evangelism. He later accepted a call to Bellevue as minister to young married adults, and Mike and Gayle moved back.

While living in Memphis they gave Joyce and Adrian two wonderful grandsons, Michael and Adrian, just seventeen months apart. "Big Adrian" and I loved having them all a part of Bellevue. But the time came when they moved to Texas and then to Atlanta. Now they come for holidays, and we go to visit them in Georgia. Michael is eighteen and Adrian is sixteen. They are tall, handsome, and gifted boys.

David and His Bride Kelly

David had committed his life to being a missionary when he was a teenager and had been on a number of summer mission trips through the years. Then he sailed with Operation Mobilization's missionary ship, the MV *Doulos,* for two years around the coasts of Spain and Africa. These were life-changing experiences for him and helped shape his life and missionary philosophy.

Adrian and I visited him three times while he was on the ship—when it was docked in Bremen, West Germany; Naples, Italy; and Lisbon, Portugal. These visits also impacted our missionary vision. God had given our son a heart for the world, and we would enter into a greater burden for the world than ever before.

David spent six months out of these two years in Spain. While he was there, God gave him a burden to return to that country to become a church planter. When he returned home from the two-year mission, David met Kelly Mason. God had been speaking to her about becoming a missionary. Their hearts and their life mission became one, and that year wedding bells again chimed in the Rogers' household. David and Kelly were among the first couples to marry in the new Bellevue worship center.

David finished his seminary training and returned to Memphis for Kelly to deliver their first son, Jonathan. When Jonathan was just seven months old, the young Rogers were commissioned as career missionaries and left for Spain, where God had led David and Kelly to minister.

This was a sad, happy occasion. The tears were flowing.

Nevertheless, God filled Adrian and me with great joy as we thought about what a blessing it was to have a son and a daughter-in-law who loved God enough to leave father and mother, houses and lands to preach the gospel to the people of Spain.

We, too, would come to love the people of Spain and go to visit as often as we could—usually once a year. Another baby boy, Stephen Paul, was born on November 22, 1996, while David and Kelly lived in Badajoz, Spain. I went to help with the baby the middle of December, and Adrian arrived on Christmas Eve. What a special time this was for Grammy and Papa. We were able to share in the baby's dedication service. Adrian preached, and David interpreted for him. They make quite a team.

Jonathan is now fifteen, and Stephen is eight. They have lived in Spain all of their lives and are fluent in both English and Spanish. We don't see them enough, but we love them greatly and are so proud of them.

JANICE AND HER GROOM BRYAN

Our youngest daughter, Janice, married her high school sweetheart Bryan Edmiston. She had gone through a great heartbreak, but God was so good to bring Bryan back into her life. He became the father to their two wonderful girls, Angela and Rachel, and then to Andrew and Breanna. God turned a great heartache into a great blessing. They all now live in Memphis, and we see them frequently.

They all enjoy going to the Mexican restaurant, El Chico's, which has become a family tradition. Angie just graduated from college with honors and is teaching school. She is married to Nathan Luce, whom we all love. Rachel just graduated from high school with honors and is studying biblical counseling.

Andrew, who is nine years old, amazed us all with his spiritual insights when he was only four years old. During the election for President in 2000, Andrew expressed concern that his Mother and Daddy would be elected to be President and wife, and he would have to move from his house and Nintendo. His mother assured him he didn't have to worry because they wouldn't be elected, but even if they were that the President could have the biggest house and the best Nintendo.

Andrew then asked, "Wouldn't that be like a king? And wouldn't that be wrong? Remember when Moses "forsook the pleasures of Egypt?"

Previously Janice had told him the story of Moses. Now, some time later, he drew this spiritual analogy.

Besides his spiritual insights, Andrew also has a great sense of humor and loves to delight his Papa with jokes. Breanna is three years old and with her sanguine personality and smile has captured her Papa and Grammy's hearts. The Edmiston family is a great joy to Adrian and me.

Miracle Days

The ministry at Bellevue presented a challenge. There had been a numerical decline for twenty years. Some of the buildings were stately but worn down. The parking was inadequate to fill the worship center with people. The auditorium that would seat almost 3,000 had only about 1,500 in attendance on a strong Sunday. It was half full. I remember telling Adrian, "At least we won't have to be in a building program." At that time we did not dream of the building program we would be challenged with in a few years.

Bellevue set a record for Sunday school attendance on May 13, 1973, only a few months after Adrian came as pastor. We had set a goal of 3,800 for "Miracle Day," higher than any attendance in the church's history. Not only did we meet that goal, but we exceeded it with 4,567 in Sunday school. This "miracle" was the precedent for glory days to come.

Adrian launched other exciting events to illustrate biblical principles of faith and victory, including "Feeding of the 5,000" in 1975 with more than 5,400 attending, and "Heaven Sunday" in 1976. Like a true New Testament church, Bellevue began to grow in numbers and spiritual depth.

There was a spirit of revival and expectancy in every service. What had been a half-full building filled to overflowing, and we added a second morning service in 1977. This was sufficient for a while, but in 1982 the growth demanded a third morning worship service.

It was obvious that the church should build a new facility. Leadership began to plan and to try to purchase adjacent property. The church had already bought additional property for parking, but it was not enough to accommodate the buildings that would be necessary.

The building committee planned as best they could to build on the twenty-four acres that the church already had. They tried to buy more property from their neighbors. The price of the adjacent property was exorbitant. Even if the land was acquired, some existing buildings would have to be demolished and still the newly built structures would not be adequate.

But then God stepped in.

CHAPTER

10

A NEW VISION
FOR BELLEVUE

In the midst of all of this Adrian and three other men went to Orlando, Fla., to look at some churches that had built large facilities. That night was a sleepless one for the pastor. He knew Bellevue was a strong and vibrant church and should consider a program similar to the growing churches they had visited.

The next morning sitting at the gate in the Orlando airport, the pastor swallowed hard and asked a question that seemed to be audacious on the surface. He asked of the other three men who were with him, "Aren't we trying to pour water uphill? Why don't we sell the midtown property and move out on Interstate 40 in the area where most of our people live and others are moving in great numbers?"

Al Childress, a greatly trusted layman, said, "Pastor, are you serious?"

The pastor answered, "I'm serious that I want us to think about it."

Then Billy Mills, another strong leader in the church and a successful real estate developer, said in an affirmation, "Pastor, it would be easier to pay for if we moved out east."

At this the pastor's heart began to beat a little faster with the thought of considering such a thing. Bellevue was an historic church and had been at her present location since 1903. The associate pastor, Bob Sorrell, was another man in the quartet. He and the pastor talked about the great challenge such a move would entail. They both found themselves almost giddy about the prospect.

What would the people think? What about our tradition and our present buildings and location? Would the "oldtimers" be supportive? Is there property available?

The endeavor would be so large that in a strange way it seemed more the will of God than an easier route. Adrian later spoke of the incredible power of an idea.

He said that when he first mentioned this to the other men, he did not know how they would respond. If they had said, "That is ridiculous or impossible," he probably would have agreed with them. He adds, "That's how many good ideas are strangled at birth. An idea many times is among the most fragile and the most powerful things in the world."

Idea Turns to Action

At that point the move was only an idea. It later became a conviction. What at first we had considered unthinkable, soon became a wise and prudent step.

He then began to discuss the matter with his inner-circle leadership. They, too, bought into the idea enough to send two men to "scout out the land." Later, the pastor dubbed Roland Maddox and Morris Mills, Caleb and Joshua.

These men found 276 acres in a prime location that could be purchased for less than a few acres in midtown would cost.

It seemed to be the will of God. Things were falling into place in the direct reverse proportion to the former difficulties. The pastor then began to discuss the idea with an enlarging circle of trusted leadership. At each level there seemed to be excited response.

The committee did research on the area, the demographics and the drive time of the membership. It was now becoming more evident that it was not a foolish idea. To the contrary, now it seemed foolish not to do it.

The time came when the idea was to be presented to the church. Up until this time the idea was only discussed among select leadership. This was to keep unfounded rumors from spreading.

The pastor announced a Sunday evening report from the building committee. By this time the local newspaper had "sniffed out" the plan and wanted to print it in the Saturday edition of *The Commercial Appeal.* When the pastor learned of their plans, he called the editor and said that the plan had not even been discussed before the membership. He asked that no story be printed in the newspaper before the church was told the specifics and had opportunity to discuss and vote on it.

The editor said, "It's too big a story, and we will not sit on it. Adrian decided to leave it in the hands of God.

He later said he prayed and "told Jesus on them."

THE VOTE TO MOVE

The people came on Sunday, having read the newspaper. They were surprised and perplexed. Adrian knew that rumors were flying and people were talking about the issue. He knew that he had to break the ice, so he stood before the people on Sunday morning and asked, "How many of you believe everything you read in the newspaper? Please lift your hand."

A ripple of laughter spread across the congregation as no one lifted a hand. The pastor said, "You come this evening, and it will all be explained to you."

That evening the sanctuary was packed to overflowing. Adrian later said, "You could not have put any more people in with a shoehorn." The committee had done its work and had anticipated every question that might come up. They had a good answer for every possible objection.

Adrian watched the mood of the congregation during the presentation. They moved from being perplexed, to being interested and finally convinced and excited.

A vote was called for and of the thousands there were only six who voted against the move. These were wonderful people who had recently purchased property near the old location so they could be nearer the church. They later were among those who gave generously toward the move. For all practical purposes, therefore, the vote was unanimous.

After the vote was taken, everyone stood and gave a thunderous applause. Adrian had been a little apprehensive and had hoped that the issue would not be divisive. When he saw the result of the vote and the great emotion of the congregation, his heart began to sing.

Now the work of planning and raising money would begin. The church that was already in a time of spiritual renewal moved up to an even higher plane. Plans were made and even more property was purchased bringing the total to almost 400 acres.

Since "Joshua and Caleb' were sent to "spy out the land," the church began to call the new location "Canaan." I wrote a chorus titled, "Claiming Our Canaan." We would sing it often in church in those days.

> *It's a brand new day claiming our Canaan*
> *It's a brand new day trusting our Lord;*
> *Onward to victory, possessing the Land*
> *Proving His Word while holding His hand.*

THE CHEST OF JOASH

Plans to raise money began. Adrian suggested that the giving begin with a world missions offering. The offering was a generous one amounting to $180,000.

The next step was to pay for the property. Adrian had a chest made that was large and beautiful with a slot in the top. He named it "The Chest of Joash" after the story of King Joash in the Bible who took an offering and placed it in a chest. Adrian then challenged the people to raise in one offering enough to purchase the new property.

It was an exciting time as the people dropped their cash gifts into the chest. Others later presented to the church jewelry, cars, property, guns, boats and other gifts of kind.

It was an amazing thing to behold. Enough money was raised and the land was paid for. It was a hallelujah time "claiming our Canaan."

CHAPTER

11

GOODBYE OLD BELLEVUE; PLANNING FOR CANAAN

Adrian felt members should remember the biblical faith that built the church in its old location and the precious memories that were a part of those buildings—weddings, funerals, baptisms, worship services, and revival meetings. He knew there needed to be an emotional transfer to the new location. This he accomplished by two means—the Stones of Remembrance and the Treasure Chest of Memories.

He held a banquet for the older people who were a part of the church—some of whom had been members for over fifty years. He told them how Joshua and the children of Israel miraculously passed over the Jordan River that God had dried up. When they were across, God told them to pick up twelve stones to remember what He had done.

Adrian asked these dear saints to go to the "riverbed of their memories" and to select twelve great principles that had made the church such a mighty force throughout its history.

In succeeding services he would have different little boys dressed in biblical attire stand next to an older member and ask, "What is this stone?" The long-time member would answer, "Son, that is the stone of faith that has helped us through the years and brought us thus far." He would go on to explain the significance of that stone and the lesson God had taught the church. We would leave the stone on the platform, and repeat the scene for each succeeding service until a mound of twelve stones lay before the congregation.

The pastor then reminded the people that it is not buildings that make up the church, but rather these great qualities and principles. Bellevue would still be Bellevue even in a different location.

We renamed the Chest of Joash as the Treasure Chest of Memories. Then the church held a pageant depicting victories, episodes and other blessings from our long history. After the pageant the congregation filed past the chest, and each participant dropped in a written memory of a personal experience or blessing.

A Designer for the New Building

We engaged a church designer from California named Darrell Howe. Adrian told him we wanted the building to be contemporary-colonial.

God inspired this man to design a magnificent building, beautiful and stately, but in keeping with the times. It has colonial-style columns and is topped with a stained glass window representing the world. At the apex, depicted on the glass, there is a lighted cross that sends out beams of light across the world.

Underneath is this Scripture I selected under the Lord's leadership, "Send out Thy light and Thy truth!" (Ps. 43:3a). Truly this pastor and this church specialize in sending forth the Light of the world and the Word of Truth—the Lord Jesus Christ.

The property, though beautiful, was located on back-country roads. The church built spacious roads through the property of neighbors who were happy to have new frontage on beautiful roads.

Adrian's heart was captured by the whole process. He often would drive out to the new location, walk through the woods and pray. He would stand where he surmised the pulpit would be located and imagine himself preaching at the new location and multitudes being saved. It was a dream that would come true.

The Groundbreaking Ceremony

The day came for the groundbreaking ceremony.

It was elaborately planned. A platform was built with risers for a great choir. The entire church family was invited along with civic leaders and dignitaries.

We chose the theme, "Claiming Our Canaan." I sang a song to fit in with the theme titled, "I Want That Mountain." It spoke of Caleb's faith that God was able to conquer Canaan, the land God had promised to give them. Caleb was an Old Testament hero who defeated giants when he was eighty years old.

The little children received yellow plastic hats that looked like construction helmets. The pastor called them "Caleb's Kids."

He had ten twelve-foot-tall giants painted on foam core board. These giants had names like "fear," "unbelief," "pride," and "prayerlessness." They were lying on the ground and could not be seen until later when they would be lifted up one by one.

The pastor stood on the platform and asked for a report from the twelve spies who had been sent to check out Canaan.

The drama department had created ten grasshopper suits. Their hind legs attached to the heel and the waist would pump up and down as they would walk. They walked up and stood in front of the pastor on the platform. The grasshoppers agreed the land was magnificent but there were giants in the land.

The pastor asked them one by one what their names were. One would answer, for example, "The giant of fear." The giant with FEAR written on his chest would be made to stand. One by one the grasshoppers would report and giants would be lifted up. When each giant was lifted up, a banner would be lifted over the choir with the opposite characteristic.

For example, when the giant of fear was presented the pastor asked the kids, "Can fear keep us out of this land?" The kids shouted, "No!" Then he asked, "What do we need instead of fear?"

Then the banner called COURAGE came up over the choir, and the kids shouted, "Courage."

All ten giants were raised and all the banners lifted. The pastor then dismissed each grasshopper to go stand by his giant and tremble. "Caleb's Kids" were near the grasshoppers and began to throw pebbles at them.

Then the pastor said, "We've heard a report from ten. Are there not others? Two men who represented Caleb and Joshua, dressed in beautiful biblical attire, came forward bringing a large cluster of grapes suspended from a pole between them.

When the pastor asked for a report, they said, "Let us go up at once. We are well able to take the land for God is with us."

The pastor then said, "Very well! Let the groundbreaking begin." The children released hundreds of multicolored balloons filled with helium. Each balloon had a Scripture verse attached. At the same time a miniature canon fired, and eighty trumpets began to blow.

Then the excitement really began. Behind a hill a deep-throated rumble was heard from the diesel engine of a mighty bulldozer that had been sequestered out of sight. The choir began to sing, "Victory in Jesus," and the bulldozer squared up with a row of ten giants before it. By then people had figured out what was about to happen, and they began to shout.

For the groundbreaking the bulldozer blade dropped and the rich soil began to curl on it. The grasshoppers fled, and one by one the giants fell.

The cheering continued as another huge earth-moving machine came from over the hill with a ten-foot banner on its side that said, "Victory in Jesus." It was electrifying. The memory was indelibly etched in the hearts of children and adults alike. For a moment we were all "Caleb's Kids."

What followed was many months of preparing ground, laying the foundation, constructing steel beams and walls. The buildings soon began to take shape.

"NEBO GAZEBO"

We constructed a gazebo on a nearby hill from which Bellevue members could view the property and buildings during construction. Adrian nicknamed it "Nebo Gazebo," to represent Mount Nebo in the Scriptures, where Moses viewed the Promised Land.

Many people enjoyed coming to this place and "viewing the land."

The Last Day at Old Bellevue

Adrian knew the last day at Old Bellevue would be both a sad and a happy time. In many ways it was like saying goodbye to an old friend. There were hugs and tears, but nothing was morose. The sadness was leaving this worship center that had served Bellevue since 1952. The joy was the grand entrance of the people into the building.

Someone described that closing day: "Although Bellevue's people were excited about the new church home God had given them, the final worship service in midtown on Sunday evening, November 12, 1989, was bittersweet."

At the conclusion of the service, after the choir had sung "Now the Day Is Over," Pastor Rogers knelt on the platform to pray, and the congregation that filled both balconies as well as the main floor remained seated and still for several minutes. A quiet but holy atmosphere saturated the place as some wept openly, and a silent flurry of flashbulbs captured the moment.

In the last *Bellevue Messenger* mailed from 70 N. Bellevue, Pastor Rogers wrote:

> This grand old building has served us well. Her halls have been filled with happy hallelujahs. Her rafters have resounded with praise. Her doors have welcomed so many seekers after God. But this is a brand new day and a grand new day. We will experience what those who have gone before us experienced when they entered this sanctuary in 1952. We will be awestruck.

CHAPTER

12

THE JOURNEY TO
NEW BELLEVUE

When the new building was completed, we transported the Treasure Chest of Memories to the new location—much like the Ark of the Covenant. We attached rods and rested them on the shoulders of four men. They took the chest on six successive days' journeys. It would rest each night in the home of a Bellevue member.

It was a thrilling experience. Church members walked day by day along with the Chest of Memories. Others carried glorious banners and walked ahead of it.

The chest arrived on the final day at the grand front gate of the new church campus. Adrian and some of our family walked this final leg of the journey. The chest rested in front of the great iron gates at the entrance to the church campus. Beyond these gates was an extended roadway that led to the entrance of the new building. The next day at the appointed time trumpets sounded from the roof of the worship center and the gates swung open wide. Already thousands of people had come in through other gates and were lining both sides of the road.

The chest—again carried by four men—moved toward the doorway. Behind the chest was Bellevue's marching band and before the chest was an array of banners.

The Bellevue choir was assembled on risers placed on the portico just before the front doors. We lifted mighty choruses of praise to God. Then from the ellipse on the front lawn a covey of white doves was released.

These feathered creatures began to swirl higher and higher into the azure blue sky.

When they were out of sight, the front doors swung open and thousands poured through them to see the spacious worship center. Then they dispersed to examine the ancillary buildings and educational space.

The pastor had wanted all of this to transpire before the inaugural worship service the next day. His desire was that the people, having already examined the new facility, could turn their attention to worship.

There were no guest speakers nor dignitaries. Adrian preached in that magnificent worship center—which he had envisioned before the foundation was laid.

He was praying that the worship center, seating approximately 7,000 would be filled. Yet provision was made for two services that morning. *Both* services were filled.

Church for All Ages

At the new location Bellevue developed an exciting program that reached all ages. One group that exceeded the others was young married adults with babies and young children. While the church thought it had prepared for the children's and nursery areas, it was soon obvious that more space was needed. So we built a 100,000-square-foot building, named the "Love Building." The church had hoped to build a family life center next, but the children's building stepped ahead.

The next building was the Family Life Center, which we called the Grace Building. The motto for the building became:

> G iving
> R ecreation
> A
> C hristian
> E mphasis

Next, we built the Fellowship Building, a spacious hall with provision for a library, a bookstore, an events registration area, an immense dining room, special meeting rooms, and more education space.

The completed projects left a quadrangle between these buildings. This space, known as the Courtyard, became a cameo. Covered walkways are on every side with magnificent columns supporting them. The grounds are carefully cared for. There are benches and outdoor furniture for people to stop and visit. Soft music is piped into the area. In the center is a bronze statue of Jesus on His knees washing Simon Peter's feet.

Our granddaughter, Angela, was the first to have a wedding reception in the new courtyard.

CHAPTER

13

BELLEVUE'S CHRIST-CENTERED MINISTRIES

Bellevue Baptist Church is unashamedly a "Jesus church." The central theme of the preaching and program of Adrian Rogers is magnifying Jesus through worship and the Word. This is the key tenet of the church's mission statement:

Magnifying Jesus through worship and the Word
Moving believers in Jesus toward maturity and ministry
Making Jesus known to our neighbors and the nations

The pastor believes a lifted-up Savior will draw people to Himself. He has refused to lower the standard with user-friendly evangelism. He believes a church needs to be seeker sensitive, but he believes that the true seeker is Jesus. Jesus has come to "seek and to save that which was lost" (Luke 19:10). That is not to say that the church should be cold and unfriendly or that unsaved persons would not be treated with dignity and respect. The pastor welcomes guests with all of his heart every Sunday.

The sermon and the invitation, however, will be about Jesus. Typical of Adrian Rogers' invitation is for him to stand behind the pulpit after he has explained salvation, lift his hands and exhort people to, "Come to Jesus."

The preaching of the written Word of God, the Bible, and lifting up Jesus, the living Word of God, have built the foundation to the ministry of Adrian Rogers. A number of ancillary ministries that complement this foundation also are a vital part of Bellevue's outreach. The music ministry was first under the leadership of Thomas P. Lane, whose tenure at Bellevue lasted for thirty-seven years. Great anthems and the singing of the Messiah were memorable moments of his ministry.

James D. Whitmire became the praise worship leader upon Tommy's retirement. Outstanding pageants known as The Singing Christmas Tree and the Memphis Passion Play have become mighty forces of outreach for Christ.

At the end of each pageant, the pastor will give an invitation to those who are not certain of their salvation to receive Christ into their hearts. They are then asked if they have done this to declare it by giving their name and checking the appropriate place on the registration form. Many of these are from different denominational persuasions and have never heard a clear gospel message, but will return to their churches having been truly saved. More than 95,000 people have prayed to receive Christ at these events.

An Enlarged Women's Ministry

In 1980 Sarah Maddox and I received our husbands' encouragement to plan a nationwide Women's Concerns Conference. It was the first of its kind in our circle of influence. We hoped for an attendance of 2,000, but 4,000 women from many states flooded the halls of old Bellevue.

In 1982 we expanded the Women's Missionary Society into a multi-faceted women's ministry, with a full time director, Velma Rhea Torbett. It became a model across the Southern Baptist Convention, growing from 200 women attending monthly meetings to an average attendance of 700 women at various weekly meetings. Marge Lenow assumed the directorship when Velma Rhea retired.

An Expanded Church-Wide Missions Program

It was our vision that the mission education and outreach of Bellevue would involve the whole church. Not only is Bellevue a Jesus church, it is a missionary church. Our participation in worldwide missions has greatly expanded and has leaped out of the walls of our buildings into all the world.

One of the most significant of these outreach programs has been a radio and television ministry which now is called "Love Worth Finding." This ministry began early in Adrian's Bellevue ministry under the name, "Word for the World."

While the church had a local radio and television ministry before our arrival, the message now extends to 2,000 radio stations each weekday, and 14,000 television outlets on the weekends. The message is broadcast into 120 nations. Adrian likes to say that the sun never sets on the ministry of "Love Worth Finding."

Another dramatic missionary outreach has been the emphasis of members taking their own time and money to go into the world with the gospel message. Many have gone on volunteer mission trips around the world.

Adrian has participated in crusades to Korea, Brazil, Argentina, and Romania. One of the most fruitful was a strategic plan to reach the Central American countries under the leadership of David Ripley, a member of Bellevue. This was a five-year plan with an outreach into almost every facet of life. There were ministries to business people as Bellevue's business leadership interacted with theirs. There were ministries to pastors and wives with conferences and special materials.

There was ministry to health needs with Bellevue's doctors and nurses who volunteered their services. There have been ministries into the schools with Bellevue's young people carrying the message to other youth. Our granddaughters Angela and Rachel were greatly impacted by these volunteer mission trips.

There have been ministries to street gangs and to those in prison. Beyond all of this "El Amor Que Vale" (the Spanish ministry of "Love Worth Finding") is broadcast regularly in Central America and is widely accepted by pastors and laity alike.

All of this has climaxed from time to time in great crusades in convention halls or sports stadiums.

Bellevue has sponsored a dynamic church in Tegucigalpa, Honduras, called Impacto Church, and has undergirded another start-up church in San Pedro Sula.

Bellevue has sent a host of career missionaries here in the United States and around the world, including our son David and his family, now ministering in Spain.

God has graciously crowned the years at Bellevue with multiplied blessings. The church membership has grown from 8,000 to 29,000 members. It is situated on 360 landscaped acres. Almost one million square feet of building space belongs to the church—debt free. The church is now able to give millions of dollars to world missions yearly ($4.1 million in 2004), in addition to self-funded missionary outreach programs of many members.

Countless souls have come to Christ through the ministry of the church—God alone knows the number.

Unexpected Ministry Opportunities

Adrian had a surprise in March 2004 that led to the upheaval of his plans. He was prepared to go to Guatemala City in Central America to preach a citywide crusade in a 30,000-seat soccer stadium, supported and promoted by a thousand local cooperating churches. His heart was beating with anticipation. But there was something that was about to happen that dealt with a heartbeat of another kind.

Three years before he had experienced a minor heart attack that resulted in a stent being inserted into a major artery to increase the blood flow. This seemed to do the job, and Adrian said at the time he felt as good as new.

But now three years later his friend and medical doctor, Mark Castellaw, recommended that he have a heart catheterization to check on the stent and its effectiveness. This was just days before the Guatemala trip. Adrian protested that he felt fine and suggested he have the procedure when he came home from the crusade. Dr. Castellaw kindly insisted that the procedure be done before leaving the United States.

Adrian eventually agreed, thinking no major problem would be discovered and he could make the trip anyway. But there *was* a major problem. The artery from the previous heart attack was now ninety percent blocked. It is the artery that doctors have nicknamed "the widow maker." Adrian was a walking time bomb, and the doctor recommended an immediate bypass surgery.

Adrian never has been given to overt worry, so he said, "Praise the Lord, let's do it." This would mean a restriction that would keep him from going to the crusade and other previously planned events, such as being a speaker at the Southern Baptist Convention, attending a conference at the White House, and making a trip to London.

Adrian looks back on the experience and says with a smile, "I notice that the world went right on without me." Not only did he learn the lesson of his own dispensability, but he also learned other lessons.

He recalls:

> I discovered how much the family of God and their outpouring of love meant to me and how it gave me strength. Their expressions of love came in many practical ways. They sent delicious food, a multitude of cards, letters, beautiful plants, and flowers. This love came from the wonderful Bellevue family and from around the world.
>
> I was out of my pulpit at Bellevue for several months and was glad to get back. My health is strong, and I am looking forward to many more years of vigorous service and life.

Further he learned a lesson in patience. Adrian says patience is a quality he does not possess by natural inclination. But he developed a new awareness of its importance in his recuperation.

He came to appreciate anew the ministry of good, faithful doctors and caring nurses. Adrian had always believed this intellectually, but now he understood this at a deeper level.

He also tells everyone that he will be forever grateful for the undying and sacrificial love of a wife who ministered to him faithfully and tenderly.

Incidentally, while in the hospital God gave him wonderful ministry opportunities. Even while others assumed the preaching responsibilities in Guatemala and at the Southern Baptist Convention, Adrian shared the gospel of Jesus with his nurses, encouraged a minister whose wife was dying, and led to Christ a young man who was living with an artificial heart, awaiting a heart transplant.

Adrian saw these things as divine appointments and is grateful to God who by His providence revealed this potentially dangerous problem and for a godly doctor who insisted on an examination that uncovered this hidden problem.

CHAPTER

14

TRANSFORMATION OF THE SOUTHERN BAPTIST CONVENTION

The Southern Baptist Convention was in many ways a cradle for the ministry of Adrian Rogers. He made his profession of faith in a Southern Baptist Church, was ordained in a Southern Baptist Church, attended a Southern Baptist college and seminary. He believed then, as he believes now, that the Southern Baptist Convention has within its ranks enough people to reach the world for Christ.

Adrian was always grateful to be a Southern Baptist; but things would happen that would grieve him and make that relationship difficult. Already mentioned in chapter three were the theological problems he found at Stetson University. At times he felt it was necessary to debate with a professor, but he saw this as a lose-lose situation. It is impertinent for a student to challenge his professor. On the other hand silence would seem to be consent.

As time went on Adrian learned more about the depth of the problem. German higher criticism had begun to creep into the seminaries and colleges. "Mom and Pop" Baptist were remote from these problems. Many who might hear of the problems would not be savant enough to understand the implications and dangers that this theology had begun to have on the schools—therefore on the pastors, and eventually on the churches.

Another problem was that the convention was a monolithic organization operated like a well-oiled machine. To raise questions or bring criticism would label one as disloyal and independently minded.

Beyond all of that was a denominational press that would give cover for any theological liberalism. This grieved the young pastor, who realized the wisdom and necessity of reading trends. A sense of frustration remained in his heart and mind. He wanted to be loyal but would also think of the contradiction this created.

He would preach against this theological liberalism and in the same service take up an offering, part of which would go to underwrite it. One experience lingered long in the heart of Adrian. In a class at Stetson University taught by an ordained Baptist minister, he heard the great historic truths of the faith demeaned over and over.

After one class Adrian gathered his courage and confronted his professor of sociology. "Sir," he asked, "Are you truly saved?"

The professor shot back with a smirk, "Probably not according to your definition of salvation."

Adrian asked, "What *is* your definition of salvation, Professor?"

And the answer came back, "Salvation to me is that experience when a man escapes the consequences of a maladjustment to his fellow man."

Adrian persisted, "What I'm asking is, if you were to die today would you go to heaven or hell?"

The ordained Baptist minister, teaching in a Baptist college, paid for with Baptist money replied, "I don't know if there *is* a heaven or hell. I've never been to either one of them."

The young preacher said to himself, "One day he *will* know."

A Transforming Moment

A transforming moment came at a national convention where an unlettered preacher was trying to have something done about some of the denominational literature that was theologically liberal. The man was untrained in parliamentary procedure and therefore was adroitly maneuvered off the platform. Someone could have come alongside him and helped him say what he was trying to say, but sadly he stepped down humiliated.

Adrian vividly remembers that moment. At first he felt angry at what had happened, but then he heard God say clearly to his heart, "Adrian, you don't have to wait until they vote for you to do right." This was a simple thought but liberating to Adrian. He determined to trust and obey God whatever the convention may do or not do.

During Ensuing Years

During the ensuing years Adrian and others offered motions and spoke to issues, but with little lasting effect on the denomination, which was then controlled by the moderate wing.

Adrian considered leaving the denomination. This would be a major step should he do so. It would require his leading his church to come out of the denomination or else resigning. But in his heart he believed something could and should be done. He used this analogy. The Southern Baptist Convention is a good old ship that has taken on much water and is slowly sinking. The choices seemed to be to abandon the ship or to man the pumps. He chose the latter and was ultimately blessed in "manning the pumps" along with others.

After the "battle for the Bible" ensued, he found out that not only had the ship taken much water but there were those beneath the deck boring holes in the hull.

THE BAPTIST FAITH AND MESSAGE FELLOWSHIP

Adrian met Bill Powell, who worked with the Southern Baptist Convention Home Mission Board. Bill had formed an organization named The Baptist Faith and Message Fellowship. He called upon Adrian and asked him to join.

By this time Adrian had a high profile in "the battle for the Bible," but Bill Powell's organization seemed radical and over the top. Adrian remembers the moment like it was yesterday. He realized he had a decision to make and wondered why some of the stalwarts of the past had not been bolder against this liberalism. So he made his decision. He said,

"Yes, you can count me as a member and use my name," At that moment he knew that he was "committing denominational suicide," but in his heart and mind he said, "So be it!"

ELECTED PRESIDENT OF THE SOUTHERN BAPTIST PASTORS' CONFERENCE

Subsequently, to his surprise, Adrian was elected as president of the Southern Baptist Pastors' Conference. He had no idea he would be nominated. This, plus Adrian's open membership in the Baptist Faith and Message Fellowship, sounded an alarm bell in the halls of Southern Baptist officialdom.

While Adrian had not thought of the idea of being president, the establishment was planning to keep him from being the president of the convention. One of the leading Baptist editors, Chauncey R. Daley, the editor of the *Western Recorder*, the Kentucky state paper, later stated while giving a lecture at Southern Baptist Theological Seminary,

> Some of us saw the rising star out of Memphis named Adrian Rogers and in my mind the most brilliant of this group and one who poses the greatest threat to the Southern Baptist Convention as we have known it. It was obvious in his Pastors' Conference speeches and his evangelism conference circuits that he was to be the king. It was also obvious to some of us that he was not the kind of king we wanted. So in 1976 when it seemed to be his time, some of us who were editors began to write and talk about the kind of leadership we wanted. ... Sullivan was nominated. He was elected. He had nothing to do with being nominated, he didn't care about being Convention president, in fact, would not accept a second year, but he was used by some of us to head off Adrian Rogers (*The Baptist Reformation* by Jerry Sutton, 2000, Broadman & Holman Publishers, Nashville, Tenn., p. 55).

The editor of the Texas state paper, *The Baptist Standard,* said in an editorial, "If Rogers is nominated for the convention president, he should decline because he is too controversial."

Adrian thought that it was somewhat amusing because if he were nominated and not elected, the matter would be moot. But if he were elected, did this editor think that the majority of Baptists had no right to choose its leadership?

These and others like them probably did as much as Adrian's conservative friends to cause the possibility of the Southern Baptist Convention presidency to be a matter of discussion and prayer for him. While he had never seriously considered the highest office in the Southern Baptist Convention, he also did not feel worthy or suited for the job. The matter was not of great concern to him, because he was assured in his mind it would never come to pass.

He knew the brand placed upon him by his membership in the Baptist Faith and Message Fellowship and thought his election to such an office was impossible. Besides that, denominational leadership held no attraction for Adrian. He saw himself as a pastor/teacher/evangelist and had no desire for any other Christian service. When he was later elected, it seemed almost ironic to him.

Meanwhile, the pot continued to boil with charges and counter charges being raised over the incipient liberalism in the denomination.

Turning the Convention Back to Its Roots

Bill Powell began to study how the denomination could be turned back to its roots. He studied the bylaws thoroughly and concluded that if conservative presidents were elected ten years in a row and each of them made consistently conservative appointments to the Committee on Committees, it could be done.

The way it worked was this—the president appoints the Committee on Committees, then the Committee on Committees chooses the Committee on Nominations.

The Committee on Nominations nominates the board members for the various agencies and the convention elects the board members. The key to all of this is a series of presidents who would appoint only iron-clad conservatives.

THE HOUSTON CONVENTION

Two of Adrian's friends, Dr. Paige Patterson and Judge Paul Pressler, asked Adrian to lunch and broached the idea of his nomination. History will show that Paul Pressler and Paige Patterson were the driving force that brought the renaissance in the convention.

When they put forth the plan, unearthed by Bill Powell, Adrian was interested, but did not think in reality it could be done. Nor did he think he should be the lead-off candidate. In a prior convention a friend had nominated Adrian without his permission, and he therefore asked that his nomination be rescinded.

In 1979 the convention was to be held in Houston, Texas. The controversy was becoming more heated. Adrian began to be pressed more and more to allow his nomination. Adrian and I, of necessity, had to discuss the matter. "Where are you on a scale of one to ten?" we would ask each other.

The number on the scale never seemed to get much above a five.

"BROTHER ADRIAN, GOD WANTS YOU TO DO THIS!"

Adrian was bombarded by many people he knew and many he did not know to allow his nomination for president. Most of these Adrian was able to deal with as being the enthusiasm of well-meaning friends. But there was one phone call that gave him considerable pause. It was from Miss Bertha Smith, one of Southern Baptists' premier missionaries and a participant in the great Shantung Revival in China.

Miss Bertha was known for her prayer life and deep walk with God. She said, "Brother Adrian, God wants you to do this."

With deep respect for Miss Bertha, Adrian began to explain to her about his present responsibilities—a large, growing church, a multi-million dollar building program and children in their teenage years.

Miss Bertha then told Adrian a story about Charles Haddon Spurgeon:

> Sometimes Spurgeon felt he was overloaded with responsibilities more than he could bear. He took his New Testament into the woods to pray and meditate. He read where the Almighty had said to Paul, "My grace is sufficient for thee." The phrase made a mighty impact on Spurgeon.
>
> He began to say to himself, "Thy grace, Lord, Thy grace, sufficient for me?" And immediately the burden was lifted.
>
> Spurgeon later said his heart was filled with joy and his mouth with laughter as he contemplated God's all-sufficient grace. Brother Adrian, God's grace is also sufficient for you.

Adrian thanked Miss Bertha, had prayer and hung up the phone. At that time he was almost afraid to let her know the impact of her words. But they remained embedded in his heart. Nevertheless, the matter was not settled. Therefore, we assumed it was not God's will for us.

The Pastors' Conference

When we arrived in Houston, Adrian and I went to the pastor's conference. As we were walking to the conference, it seemed like someone was encouraging Adrian to run for president at almost every step of the way. One of these was an evangelist named Freddie Gage, who had been active in encouraging conservatives to attend the convention. He stopped Adrian on the street corner and asked him, "You're going to do it, aren't you?"

Adrian replied, "Freddie, God would have to write it in the sky."

Freddie said, "Very well, I'll rent a skywriting airplane if that's what it takes." Adrian laughed good-naturedly and went on his way.

Adrian was to preach on Monday night at the pastors' conference. The air was filled with electricity. Dr. W. A. Criswell was to bring the message following Adrian's sermon.

The two were chatting on the platform when Dr. Criswell said, "Lad, you need to let us nominate you."

"Dr. Criswell, I don't believe that's what God wants me to do," Adrian said.

Then on the heels of that conversation Dr. Criswell told that crowd, "This will be a great convention if for no other reason than to elect Adrian Rogers as our president." With these words people stood and cheered.

Oddly, Adrian and I had differing reactions to his statement. Adrian felt Dr. Criswell's statement was presumptuous, while it made me ponder these things in my heart.

"IF YOU CHANGE YOUR MIND, I WANT TO COME"

Our twenty-three year old daughter, Gayle, was our only child at home at the time we left for the convention. David was on an overseas missions trip, Janice was at youth camp and Steve was married and lived in Florida. So Gayle said, "If you change your mind about running for president of the convention, call and let me know. Because if you do, I want to come." We agreed.

A friend, Juanita Dormer, said she would come with Gayle. Unbeknownst to us, Juanita had made tentative airline reservations— just in case.

MONDAY EVENING AFTER THE PASTORS' CONFERENCE

After the pastors' conference we went back to the convention hotel where a seminary professor from Mid America Baptist Seminary told Adrian that he had a message for him from Dr. Charles Culpepper. The names of Charles Culpepper and Bertha Smith, who has already been mentioned, had been enshrined in the hearts of Southern Baptists as people of holiness. They had been in the great Shantung revival at the same time.

The message from Dr. Culpepper was this, "Tell Adrian that I have been with God, and he should allow his nomination." The impact of these words on Adrian's heart was strong. The matter seemed to be getting more and more perplexing.

We felt we needed some quiet time, so we went out for a long, leisurely dinner by ourselves. We were coming into the doors of the hotel when we met Dr. Jerry Vines and Dr. Paige Patterson. They asked, "Where have you been? We have been looking for you. Are you going to allow your nomination?"

Adrian said, "It is not settled in my heart."

These two godly men said, "Then let us go up to your room and pray." We agreed.

By now it was approaching midnight on Monday night and the election was to be on Tuesday afternoon. I joined in as the three men kneeled on the floor and fervently prayed. After an extended time of prayer, Dr. Patterson began to weep. Adrian looked up at me propped up in bed, and there was a defining moment. I held up ten fingers. With that Adrian said, "I will do it."

BACK HOME IN MEMPHIS

First thing Tuesday morning I said, "We have to call Gayle. We told her she could come if we changed our minds." So we made the call and found out that she had already packed a suitcase. She and Juanita left almost immediately. I wondered if the girls would make it in time.

BACK AT THE CONVENTION

There was an unbelievable whirlwind of activities that morning getting prepared for the events of the day. Word about Adrian's nomination had gone through the hall, and there was a "buzz." Dr. Homer Lindsey, Sr., a

Southern Baptist statesman, was asked to nominate Adrian. To do this he had to lay his reputation on the line.

There were at least four men who were nominated that morning. One was Bill Self, a lifetime friend, who had lined up with the moderate faction. At that time he held the high-profile office of president of the Foreign Mission Board. Another nominee was Dr. Robert Naylor, distinguished president emeritus of the gigantic Southwestern Baptist Theological Seminary in Ft. Worth, Texas. The fourth nominee was Judge Abner McCall, president of Baylor University, the largest Baptist University in the world.

The nominations and balloting took place.

ELECTED ON THE FIRST BALLOT

As they were calling out the results, I said to Adrian, "I don't guess Gayle is going to make it."

When the votes were counted, Adrian was elected on the first ballot. At the exact moment when her Daddy was declared the winner, I looked out over the crowd, and Gayle and Juanita were standing in a rear door of the convention hall. They had made it just in time.

It was unusual for anyone to be elected on the first ballot with more than two nominees in the contest. No one was likely to have a majority, so there would normally be a run-off election. Even more amazing was a first-ballot election in Texas, with two of Texas' favorite sons having been nominated.

Adrian was stunned. It seemed too much for him to take in. Could it be that he was president of the largest evangelical denomination in the world? There was joy on the faces of many and bewilderment on the faces of others.

A HOSTILE PRESS CONFERENCE

Adrian was little prepared for what was about to happen. He was ushered into the press room and faced a battery of editors, religion writers, and some secular news reporters. He sat in front of a forest of microphones. The questions flew—many of them hostile. Adrian later said he felt like "a piece of red meat in the midst of a pack of wild dogs."

One of the questions dealt with his relationship to Mid America Baptist Theological Seminary in Memphis, which was based on the inerrant Word of God. Adrian replied, "My friends are my friends. No election will change that."

Gayle joined us for the press conference and other activities. We were glad she got to come. We had a king sized bed, so she spent the night with us in that big bed, and we talked and told jokes until we finally fell asleep.

WELCOME HOME

We got in touch with Janice at youth camp. The youth leaders brought her home, so she could meet us at the airport. They brought her onto the plane to greet us, then we along with Gayle and Janice exited together. We were surprised to see the airport lobby filled with cheering Bellevue members. Tommy Lane, the Bellevue minister of music, led in singing a hymn of praise and Virginia Bailey, the wife of the associate pastor, presented me with two dozen long-stemmed, red roses.

Adrian, our two daughters, and I made our way to the curb where a limousine was waiting to take us home. Then we realized that there was a police escort to lead us through the city. This was exciting but made us feel a little self-conscious.

It was almost bewildering to us, but it was not without humor. When we arrived at home and the entourage pulled away, we sat with Gayle and Janice in the empty house and looked at one another. The whirlwind of activity had suddenly ceased. The four of us had a big laugh.

A Momentous but Chilling Day

The following Sunday was a momentous one at Bellevue, but there was a chilling element in it. The church was proud of its pastor/president and turned out in great numbers. They brought our family to the platform and presented me with a gorgeous bouquet of flowers. The song service centered in hymns of praise to God for what He had done.

At the appointed time Adrian stood to preach and was in the middle of his message when a side door near the pulpit burst opened and a young man with a shock of black hair and a black beard bounded onto the platform. He was barefooted and his shirt was unbuttoned down to the waist. He let out a maniacal yell and kicked over a large vase of flowers sitting on the platform. He then headed toward Adrian.

Adrian later related what went through his mind at that moment. It seemed to him as if God had spoken a whole paragraph in a split second. He felt God speaking to him and saying, "Adrian, do not be afraid. You are my man, and the devil is about to make a fool of himself." A peace came over him.

The young man brushed past Tommy Lane and flailed at him as he headed for the pastor. Adrian found himself face to face with this wild-looking individual. The man stopped, however, several feet in front of the pastor. Adrian later said, "It seemed as if this man had hit a Plexiglas shield. He was reminded of the Scripture that said, "The angel of the Lord encamps all around those who fear Him" (Ps. 34:7a, NKJV).

At that moment a choir member, Leonard Garland, a former golden gloves boxing champion, vaulted over the choir railing and struck this man with a mighty left hook to his jaw. It did its work. The man was flattened.

Then three or four men rushed to the platform and pinned him down. A young man who was a body builder and a black belt karate expert, jumped out of the balcony to the platform. As he was taking off his coat he said, "Let me at him. I'll kill him."

The pastor said, "No, please stand back."

Throughout this, God was giving Adrian a supernatural calmness. One can imagine the fear and perplexity in the congregation. Little ladies who had come to worship were not prepared for this.

I was seated between Gayle and Janice. We did not know what was happening on the platform because the pulpit was blocking our view. Gayle, moved forward so she could see; Janice was fearful because the pulpit hid her Daddy, who was kneeling on one knee beside his assailant. I put my arm around Janice and encouraged her to "plead the blood of Jesus."

Adrian laid his hand upon this man, who was still being held down, and said, "Satan, I resist you in the name of Jesus."

At that moment the man said, "Make them stop. They are killing me."

Adrian felt that the young man cringed at the name of Jesus and the mention of His blood.

Adrian felt a rush of joy because he knew where the battle was and where the victory was. Again Adrian prayed, "In the name of Jesus," asking God to bind any demonic force. At this prayer the attacker went completely limp and heaved a sigh. Adrian said to the men who were holding him down, "Release him and stand him up."

They asked, "Are you sure?"

The pastor answered, "Yes."

The man stood this time face to face with the pastor with a docile spirit. Adrian embraced him and said to him, "God loves you, and so do we." He then asked the men to lead the young man out, and he went quietly. Adrian felt it was a face-to-face encounter with evil and that God had confirmed his word to Adrian's heart when He said, "Don't be afraid. You're my man, and the devil's about to make a fool of himself."

Adrian wanted to finish his sermon, but he knew at that moment the congregation was not ready for the second half of his message. He asked Tommy Lane to sing again a song that had already been sung earlier, "To God Be the Glory." It seemed as if the breath of heaven blew through the congregation, and Adrian completed his message. At the invitation time a great many people responded.

The entire episode was telecast live because the cameras were kept rolling. The matter became the subject of community interest and concern as the situation was played over and over on various television stations.

God used it to bring many under conviction and encourage them to stand for Jesus.

A Visit to the Oval Office

The following year was filled with excitement. There was a never-to-be-forgotten visit for Adrian, Janice and me with the President of the United States, Jimmy Carter, in the Oval Office. The visit, however, would later be the source of some contention. President Carter had aligned himself with the moderate faction of the convention.

At one of their meetings he said Adrian Rogers asked him why didn't he turn from secular humanism to biblical faith. Adrian was certain that he had not said this to the President. He knew that if he had done such a thing, it would be indelibly etched in his mind. He wrote to President Carter and said, "I did not call you a secular humanist; nor do I believe you are one. While we may differ in denominational politics and theological views, I have been grateful for your open declaration of your faith in Jesus."

Jimmy Carter wrote back a hand written letter, "I know that is what you said, because it was the first time I had ever heard the term *secular humanism*. Rosalyn and I discussed it. But if you would like to talk about it further, I am willing."

Subsequently, Adrian made a trip to Atlanta, Ga., to the Carter Center and talked at length to the former President. He told Jimmy Carter face to face that he did not think he was a secular humanist, and even if he did, he would not have the impertinence and "cheek" to say such a thing while in the Oval Office.

Then he said to the President, "I do remember saying while leaving the office, 'We need to take a stand for Christ and turn this nation away from secular humanism.'"

Then he said, "President Carter, you know there's often what a man says and what he thinks he said and what a man hears and what he thinks he heard."

The President said, "You are a very persuasive person." The two shared theological views over a glass of grapefruit juice.

Presidential Duties—Like Having Another Job

Adrian has since likened being president of the Southern Baptist Convention to another job superimposed on your regular job. He realized that he had much to learn—the denomination organization and its leadership, the issues that were before the convention in many areas of life, the constitution and by-laws of the convention, and Roberts' Rules of Order.

Adrian had a sinking feeling when it dawned on him that he would have to attend every session in the coming year and even more—pay attention.

Adrian performed his duties as the president, made his appointments based on the appointees' allegiance to the Word of God and presided over the annual meeting in Saint Louis, Mo., in June 1980.

DECLINING A SECOND TERM

In February 1980 Adrian had his gall bladder removed. His recuperation was nominal, but while he was in the hospital he began to consider what his priorities for the coming year should be. The church was in the middle of our large building program, and he had teenagers still at home. These were important years of their lives.

He felt it was not necessary for him to run for the almost automatic second term of president of the convention. History would show that that decision would be significant in the unfolding of the drama of the "battle for the Bible" in the Southern Baptist Convention.

The moderates had planned to take the convention leadership back after Adrian's second term. The reason for their hopes was that the convention was to be held in Los Angeles, away from the Bible belt. Many in the Southern Baptist heartland would not be able to attend, especially those in rural churches. But Adrian's decision not to seek a second term threw the moderates' plan out of synchronization. Dr. Bailey Smith, a staunch conservative, was elected to replace him at the St. Louis convention.

A series of conservative leaders followed, and the battle heated up. Dr. Charles Stanley was elected president in 1984 and presided over the convention that met in Dallas in 1985. This is significant because Baylor University would go all out to deny Charles Stanley a second term. Texas was the logical place to do this. The biggest convention in the history of the Southern Baptist Convention took place at the Dallas Convention Center. Some 45,000 attended.

Baylor had been a dominant force in Texas Baptist life for many decades. Her alumni were strategically placed across the state. They had been networked to be present to unseat Charles Stanley. They had chosen as their champion Dr. Winfred Moore, the affable pastor of the First Baptist Church of Amarillo, Texas. Winfred Moore would be a formidable opponent to Stanley. He was a Texan with a strong church known for its denominational support. He boasted of being a conservative, yet he lined up with the liberal/moderate faction. This seemed the perfect time for the moderates—the Baylor machine, the Texas turf, and a favorite son.

Charles Stanley was elected by a narrow margin, and Winfred Moore was subsequently elected first vice president. There seemed to be a crack in the conservative rock. It was said that Winfred Moore would be easily elected in Atlanta in 1986. The conservatives were now challenged to find a candidate to succeed Stanley and defeat Winfred Moore.

Thirty conservatives met in Atlanta to discuss the matter. Adrian was among them. By this time he was weary of the battle and felt it was taking away time and energy from the main cause of soul winning and church building. He told his fellows, "It seems like all we are contending for is real estate and organizations."

Paige Patterson countered: "That is not so. If we can be successful, we will have everything in place to touch the world for Jesus Christ.

In his heart Adrian knew this was so.

A secret ballot was taken as to who should be the next candidate. Each man wrote a name on a slip of paper, folded it and passed it in. All of them came back with Adrian's name except for one piece of paper— the one Adrian turned in. Adrian took the challenge and allowed his name to be placed before the convention in Atlanta, knowing that the moderate forces and Winfred Moore would be strong opposition. Adrian was, however, elected president with a strong margin.

THE PEACE COMMITTEE

Another outcome of the Dallas convention was the formation of a committee that came to be called The Peace Committee. This committee of twenty-two people consisted of high-profile conservatives, high-profile liberals, and some who were not aligned.

This committee met fifteen times in the next two years. It was their assignment to ferret out the cause of the denominational division and to make recommendations to the convention for ways to solve the problems.

Adrian calls this, "one of the most challenging and sometimes exhilarating times of my life. The exhilaration did not mean pleasure as such, but an experience that called upon my every faculty—mental, emotional and spiritual. The debate was intense, but it was done in a controlled atmosphere."

NO COMPROMISE

Adrian felt this was a battle for the heart and soul of Southern Baptists, and in some ways all evangelicals. He made up his mind to stand firm for the inerrancy of the Scriptures no matter what.

A successful lawyer who represented the moderate faction pulled Adrian aside and said, "Adrian, if you don't compromise, we will never get together."

Adrian replied, "I'm willing to compromise about many things, but not the Word of God. So far as getting together is concerned, we don't have to get together. The Southern Baptist Convention, as it is, does not have to survive. I don't have to be the pastor of Bellevue Baptist Church. I don't have to be loved; I don't even have to live. But I will not compromise the Word of God."

The Turnaround of the Southern Baptist Convention

After two years of the committee's face-to-face debating, a report was worked out that would be presented to the next annual meeting. This report concluded that the division in the convention was primarily over doctrinal issues, especially the nature of the Bible. The report came down firmly on the side of biblical inerrancy. The moderates resisted to the end, but they did not prevail.

Adrian presided at the annual meeting when the report was given and confirmed by a great majority of those present. That seemed to be the final straw that broke the back of the moderate/liberal position in the convention.

Conservative presidents continued to be elected, and the boards and agencies began to be filled with those who took a strong stand for the inerrancy of the Bible. The unthinkable had happened. The dictum of history is that institutions and organizations that move to the left never turn around. Usually new entities must be raised up to stand for conservative causes. But now the gigantic Southern Baptist Convention had turned back to its roots and its once-solid biblical stance.

Adrian feels his part in the matter was and is one of the most significant episodes in his life and ministry. Even his detractors recognized Adrian's part in the transformation of the Convention. Moderate historians, Walter B. Shurden and Randy Shepley, wrote:

> I sincerely doubt ... that fundamentalism could have known its measure of success apart from Adrian Rogers. Three times the president of the SBC in a span of nine years, he was crucial in the pro-fundamentalist outcome of the Peace Committee. No other fundamentalist could

rival him as preacher, debater, or intransigent believer. When the leadership of the fundamentalists met for their strategy sessions, the press releases often read, "Adrian Rogers presided." He was by far fundamentalists' most capable leader and moderates' most formidable opponent" (*Going for the Jugular*, Mercer University Press, 1996, Macon, Ga., p. 276).

Busy Years of Influence

These years were busy. Adrian and I traveled overseas to visit Southern Baptist mission outreaches, first stopping in Mexico City, then traveling to Brazil, Zimbabwe, and finally Nairobi, Kenya.

Probably the most interesting and stirring visit was with missionary, Jimmy Hooten. He took us through the bush where we saw wildebeests, giraffes, ostriches, gazelles, and zebras; then he brought us to visit with Christian Massai natives. We sat with them on three-legged stools in a dung hut and drank coffee. We still pray for these fellow believers.

During this time Adrian was able to consult with and give advice to three American presidents, Jimmy Carter, Ronald Reagan and George Herbert Walker Bush. Since then, he has had quality time with George W. Bush in the Oval Office and other venues.

A STATE DINNER IN THE ROSE GARDEN

The most memorable of these events was when Adrian and I received an invitation to a state dinner hosted by Ronald and Nancy Reagan in the Rose Garden.

We felt self-conscious as other invited guests and dignitaries rolled up to the White House in black shiny limousines. We had rented a taxi, which was not allowed on the White House grounds, so we walked the last half block. No one had instructed us in proper protocol.

We marveled that we would ever be able to attend such an event. We thought of the Scripture that declares, "A man's gift makes room for him, and brings him before great men" (Prov. 18:16, NKJV).

Adrian was dressed appropriately in a tuxedo, and I was in a gown. As we stepped inside the White House, we were greeted. Then a handsome young marine escorted me up the stairs, as Adrian walked behind. When we came to a large reception room filled with many dignitaries, the marine announced, "Dr. and Mrs. Adrian Rogers." There were entertainers, sports luminaries, successful business people, and political shakers and movers. Adrian and I felt out of place and backed up against the wall and began to talk to one another. It was then that we spotted at least one friendly face, the only other clergyman present. He also lived in Memphis and was the president of his convention.

There was then a formal receiving line where President Reagan and the First Lady greeted the guests. Soon after we passed through the line, we were greeted by Vice President George Bush and his wife, Barbara. The Bushes asked if they could accompany Adrian and me down to the Rose Garden. What an honor that was!

It was a perfect summer evening in Washington. A beautiful moon was out and a string quartet was playing. The Rose Garden was planted with all white flowers and suspended from the trees were magnificent white Japanese lanterns. It was all so elegant—almost breathtaking!

Adrian and I were seated at separate tables as is the custom for such events. Adrian found himself seated at a table with Barbara Bush at his right hand, whom he found to be warm and engaging and often humorous. He knew all of this was a once-in-a-lifetime experience. Even the salad was festooned with edible flowers.

I was seated at another table next to a man who worked with Radio Europe. Although I was clearly out of my comfort zone, I mused later that this man probably felt just at as much a lack of words as I did, when he heard that my husband was a Baptist preacher and president of the Southern Baptist Convention. However, it was a pleasant evening and a never-to-be-forgotten occasion.

After the dinner had ended, there was a party with well-known entertainers on the program. It was interesting to circulate among the guests and see the President standing with others telling jokes and making everyone feel welcome.

The party went on until the late hours of the night. When we decided it was time for us to leave, we had no limousine awaiting us, like some of the others. So in an un-ceremonial way, we walked out of the front door of The White House. Once past the front gate, Adrian hailed a cab.

We knew we had re-entered the "real world."

A FLIGHT TO REMEMBER

Another exciting episode for Adrian was an amazing flight on Air Force One. During a visit with President George H. W. Bush in the Oval Office, President Bush said, "I am flying to Memphis tomorrow, and I would like you to be my guest on Air Force One."

Adrian said, "Mr. President, I had planned to go back to Memphis today."

The President replied, "If you change your mind, call this number and let us know." Adrian thought, I would be a fool to pass up this opportunity. So he made the call, bought a toothbrush and a razor, and secured a room at the Holiday Inn.

The next morning when he appeared at The White House, he was escorted to a garage beneath the premises. In the van were the driver, the man who plans and choreographs trips for the President, and the President's War Advisor, who carries a device known as the "football" that would be used to launch a nuclear attack if it would ever be necessary.

Adrian, as usual, was full of questions.

The van arrived at Anderson Air Force Base and drove past the guards without any security check. Adrian looked up and there—gleaming in the sun—was Air Force One. He was all eyes as he went up the steps into this magnificent aircraft.

He noticed the President's office as he passed to the first class section. On the first seat in the first class section was a beautifully lettered card that said, "Dr. Adrian Rogers." Adrian would be sitting beside the President's personal physician.

Farther back were members of Congress. Then a section for the press and yet farther back was a contingent of Secret Service agents. Adrian walked toward the back of the plane to take it all in. He was impressed with the Secret Service agents who had removed their coats. He could see their weapons.

The President came aboard, waved to everyone, and went to his office.

The plane lifted off. After it reached altitude, a steward came to Adrian and said, "The President would like for you to come to his office."

The two drank coffee and had a pleasant, interesting conversation. Adrian thought, *I, most likely, will never have an opportunity like this again.* He wished for a photograph of the event. About that time the door opened and a photographer stepped in to make a picture of Adrian and the President.

Later, Adrian received the picture with a note from the President. It was inscribed: "To Adrian Rogers with great pride in your dedicated Christian service and with warm personal regards. George Bush."

Adrian cherishes the picture and this unparalleled opportunity.

"I Am a Companion of All Them that Fear Thee"

While Adrian was a leader in the Southern Baptist Convention, he understood that the Kingdom was bigger than his denomination. He fellowshipped and worked with others who believed in the Lordship of Christ and the inerrancy of Scripture (although some may not have believed the finer points of theology that Adrian taught).

From time to time he has felt led to get out of his own denominational boundaries as far as he could without compromising his convictions. The Scripture says, "I am a companion of all them that fear Thee and of them that keep Thy precepts" (Ps. 119:63). Adrian has felt that he can be a partner with any God-fearing, Bible-believing person.

When Adrian and I met Bill and Vonette Bright in 1968, a warm friendship was formed. Adrian learned much about evangelism from Campus Crusade, headed by Bill and Vonette.

In 1992, shortly after the implosion of Soviet Communism, Dr. Bright invited Adrian and me to go with his organization for a crusade in Moscow. The plan was to have various speaking engagements and venues across Moscow. It was to climax with a great concert and preaching event in Red Square. Planners built a $30,000 stage, invited special musicians, and assembled a 300-voice choir from the United States and Russia.

This program was telecast on Russian national television. It was a thrill for Adrian to speak through an interpreter to many thousands of people. He thought, *Can this be? Am I truly in Red Square in Moscow preaching the gospel on nationwide television?*

The Russians were receptive and a great number professed faith in Christ in what previously had been known as an atheistic country. The people were so happy to receive the many thousands of Bibles the group distributed.

During a conversation in the Cosmos Hotel in Moscow, Adrian suggested Bill call a nationwide meeting to pray for America. And so, the three-day Fasting and Prayer conferences were born. Adrian believes these were transformational. While participants were of various doctrinal persuasions, they all believed in the Lordship of Jesus, the inerrancy of Scripture, and prayer. Adrian again caught a glimpse of the wideness of "the Kingdom."

Another dramatic event was "Washington for Jesus" held on the threshold of the 1980 presidential election. Leaders who felt that America was at a crossroad called the rally and invited Adrian to be a keynote speaker. The event was momentous with an estimated crowd of some 500,000 from various denominational backgrounds united for the cause of Christ and revival in America.

CHAPTER

15

THE BROADCASTING MINISTRY

Adrian has always been interested in broadcasting the gospel. As a college student, he went to radio station WARN in Fort Pierce, Fla., and purchased thirty minutes of broadcasting time out of his own pocket. It was heard on Sunday afternoons and was called "The Closer Walk Hour." The program managed to pay for itself with contributions.

He had obtained a reel-to-reel recorder and had a 45 rpm record player that he used to put together the makeshift program. Little did he dream that with this meager beginning so many years later he would be inducted into the National Religious Broadcasters' Hall of Fame.

"DAYBREAK"

When Adrian graduated from seminary and went to Fort Pierce, Fla., he continued in religious broadcasting. He had a daily fifteen-minute devotional program called "Daybreak." The townspeople, not familiar with his face, would recognize his voice.

"THE MERRITT ISLAND PULPIT"

In Merritt Island a radio ministry continued and others began to ask for tapes of the messages Adrian had preached. He was not enthusiastic about this, because he wanted to edit them before they went out.

One of the deacons at Merritt Island spoke to me about getting the messages recorded for distribution. I encouraged Adrian to make a "demo" tape. Then I told him, "If people were blessed the first time they heard the message, others will be blessed hearing it on tape." Adrian finally relented, and "The Merritt Island Pulpit" tape ministry was born.

Bellevue's Media Ministry

When Adrian came to Bellevue, some of the laity wanted to continue the tape ministry. The church already had a local morning television program on the ABC affiliate, channel 13, and was broadcasting the evening services on radio. The morning services were telecast live and proved a great outreach as many responded to Adrian's message.

"WORD FOR THE WORLD"

Soon there were those who encouraged an expansion of the television ministry outside the local area. A fledgling ministry was born in 1985 which we initially called "Word for the World." A layman, Buck Jones, became the director. This ministry began to grow and receive wide acceptance. In 1987 we changed the name of the ministry to "Love Worth Finding."

Upon Buck Jones' retirement in 1991, Bill Skelton came on board. The ministry began to enlarge its facilities and grow by adding stations— both radio and television.

During this time Adrian was president and Bill Skelton was executive vice president of the ministry. Because of pressing responsibilities Adrian asked Roland Maddox, a deacon and long-time friend, to take his place as president in 2002; Adrian became chairman of the board.

"LOVE WORTH FINDING"

The ministry continued to grow. At this writing "Love Worth Finding" can be heard daily on more than 2,000 radio stations and on Sundays on more than 14,000 television outlets domestically, it also is carried on eight satellites reaching 150 countries. A beautiful facility is home to the ministry where more than fifty full-time employees and about the same number of volunteers work. The ministry has taken on a size and proportion Adrian could never have dreamed.

The program is now dubbed into Spanish as *"El Amor Que Vale."* It airs in Central and South America, Spain, and many parts of the United States. "Love Worth Finding" is telecast in Israel and other Middle Eastern countries, with Arabic subscripts, where it has a large audience. The program also is available across the world via the Internet.

Love Worth Finding Ministries has received some of the National Religious Broadcasters' highest awards. In 1989 "Love Worth Finding" received the Television Broadcast Ministry of the Year, and in 2001 it received the Radio Program of the Year and the Milestone Award for fifty years of continuous broadcasting on radio.

Adrian was inducted into the National Religious Broadcasting Hall of Fame in 2002.

The Adrian Rogers Pastor Training Institute

Adrian always has had a great love for fellow pastors. Many have asked to spend time with him discussing preaching, leadership and church growth. This constant demand caused Adrian to form a non-profit organization called The Adrian Rogers Pastor Training Institute, a division of Love Worth Finding Ministries.

He feels a stewardship obligation to share what God has taught him through years of ministry. He realizes that he needs to pass it on. He describes it much like a relay race where a baton is handed from one runner to another. There is a place in the relay race where the first runner is side-by-side with the next. This is called the "transfer zone." Adrian realizes this is where he is in his ministry. He wants to help younger preachers "win their races."

Adrian enlisted our son, Steve, gifted in organization and leadership skills, to head this ministry. At this writing only a few Pastor Training Institutes have been held. They have been met with great success and enthusiasm.

A special feature of The Pastor Training Institute is a parallel conference that I lead for pastors' wives.

We believe as we enter our retirement from Bellevue, we're actually on the threshold of seeing this dynamic and helpful ministry expand in its usefulness for God's kingdom.

CHAPTER

16

MEN WHO HAVE INFLUENCED MY LIFE

As Adrian looks back on his life and ministry he says,

> I had no specific mentor, but my life and ministry have been enriched by the following men: John R. Rice, Hyman Appleman, Billy Graham, W.A. Criswell, Robert G. Lee, B. Gray Allison, Vance Havner, Major Ian Thomas, Stephen Olford, J. Sidlow Baxter, and Dr. Bill Bright.

Here is Adrian's description of each of these men.

Dr. John R. Rice, evangelist; editor, *Sword of the Lord*

When I was a young preacher, the writing and ministry of independent evangelist and editor John R. Rice, touched me. I subscribed to Dr. Rice's paper, *The Sword of the Lord* and was convicted by his clear, courageous stand on the Word of God.

At that time, John Rice was criticized and looked down on by denominational leadership because he was an independent and not afraid to critique the denomination in areas where criticism was justified. Dr. Rice really was a tenderhearted man who had a great heart for prayer and evangelism.

I bought Dr. Rice's book *Prayer, Asking and Receiving*. I devoured that book, and to this day it continues to impact my life.

HYMAN APPLEMAN, EVANGELIST

Another evangelist who had a part in molding my preaching was Hyman Appleman. He was a Jew born in White Russia and had a degree in law. He was dramatically converted and was used to bring thousands to Christ.

I read his books of sermons and was influenced by his style of preaching. A powerful preacher, he would alliterate his messages, use extensive vocabulary, and create deeply moving illustrations.

DR. BILLY GRAHAM, BILLY GRAHAM EVANGELISTIC ASSOCIATION

While I was a freshman in college, I heard Billy Graham bring a radio message on a Sunday afternoon. I asked, "Who is that?"

A friend answered, "That's Billy Graham who is leading great evangelistic crusades." My heart quickened as I heard him speak with a dynamism, authority, and forcefulness like I never heard. I learned that Billy Graham would be speaking at a factory within driving distance of the university. I determined to hear him and hopefully meet him. I did meet him and had my picture taken with him. It is one of my "treasures."

Billy Graham had recently been in the Oval Office and had spoken with President Eisenhower. After that meeting I hardly wanted to wash my hands, thinking I had shaken the hand of the man who had shaken the hand of the President of the United States. A relationship later developed that has lasted over fifty years.

I hold Billy Graham as a hero and am grateful to call him my friend. It was my privilege to speak in Dr. Graham's conference center, The Cove, to be a guest in his home, and to spend extensive time of prayer with him.

DR. ROBERT G. LEE, FORMER PASTOR, BELLEVUE BAPTIST CHURCH, MEMPHIS

Another who influenced my life was Dr. Robert G. Lee, former pastor of Bellevue Baptist Church in Memphis. I first heard Dr. Lee preach at First Baptist Church in West Palm Beach when I was in high school. I still remember his sermons, "Is Hell a Myth?" and "Pay Day Some Day." I

Adrian's School Pictures: Above in first
grade; below in fourth grade

Above: Adrian's mother, Rose.
Below, Arden D. Rogers, with sons
"Buddy" *(left)* and Adrian *(right).*

DAYS AT PALM BEACH HIGH SCHOOL
WEST PALM BEACH, FLA.;   1947-1950

Most Likely to Succeed

Clockwise from top:
Captain of the team and voted "Most
Valuable Back"; "I'll always cheer you
on!"; voted by classmates "Most
Likely to Succeed"; Joyce and Adrian
high school graduation, 1950.

MARRIED TO JOYCE GENTRY
SEPT. 2, 1951

Above right: Gayle, Steve and Baby
Philip,1958.
Left, Adrian with Janice and David in a
snowstorm, 1968. **Below:** Steve (10), Gayle (8),
Janice (3), David (4), 1964.

COLLEGE YEARS, FIRST BAPTIST CHURCH, FELLSMERE, FLA. 1951-1954

Above: Adrian's first baptism.
Below, Joyce and Adrian with Joyce's father, Guston C. Gentry

Left, Seminary pastorate, Waveland Baptist Chapel, Waveland, Miss., 1955-1958.

Middle: Park View Baptist Church, Fort Pierce, Fla., 1958-1964.
Lower left: Two thousand people formed a "Living Cross" at First Baptist Church, Merritt Island, Fla., pastored 1964-1972.

BELLEVUE BAPTIST
CHURCH,
MEMPHIS, TENN.

Bellevue's New Pastor Inspires Sudden Growth

THE COMMERCIAL APPEAL MEMPHIS SATURDAY MORN.

The Rev. Adrian Rogers

Top: Three
pastors of
Bellevue: Dr.
Robert G. Lee,
Dr. Ramsey
Pollard, Dr.
Adrian Rogers.
Middle: Singing
Christmas Tree.
Lower right:
Body of Christ
Day, 1981.

ELECTED THREE TIMES AS
PRESIDENT OF THE
SOUTHERN BAPTIST
CONVENTION:

1979-1980
1986-1987
1987-1988

Below: Bellevue celebrates
election of its pastor as
president. Beside Adrian are
Joyce and daughters Gayle
and Janice.

The Atlanta Journal

WEDNESDAY EVENING, JUNE 11, 1986

Rogers taking helm
of Southern Baptists

BELLEVUE BAPTIST CHURCH—WORSHIP CENTER; CORDOVA LOCATION, 2000 APPLING RO

Groundbreaking for New Location of Bellevue
Claiming Our Canaan, July 19, 1987

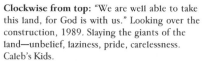

Clockwise from top: "We are well able to take this land, for God is with us." Looking over the construction, 1989. Slaying the giants of the land—unbelief, laziness, pride, carelessness. Caleb's Kids.

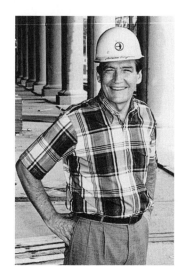

Above: Front of new building Bellevue Baptist
Church, Cordova, Tenn., "Send out Thy Light and
Thy Truth" (Ps. 43:3). **Below:** Baptizing
granddaughter, Rachel Edmiston, 1992;
Right: Joyce and Adrian, Bellevue courtyard 2003.

To Dr. Adrian Rogers
With best wishes,

Ronald Reagan

Above: President Ronald Reagan signing National Day of Prayer Proclamation, 1987, with Vonette Bright, Pat Boone, White House Aide, Adrian Rogers, Richard Halverson. **Below:** Adrian, speaker at National Day of Prayer at the White House, with President George W. Bush, May 3, 2001.

Clockwise from top left:
Attending the inauguration of President George H. W. Bush, Jan. 20, 1989. Aboard "Air Force One with President George H. W. Bush, Nov, 22, 1989. In the Oval Office with President Jimmy Carter, daughter Janice and wife, Joyce, 1979. With The Honorable Gordon England *(left)*, Secretary of the Navy, General Michael W. Hagee *(right)*, 33rd Commandant of the Marine Corps at National Cathedral, Washingdon, DC, where Adrian spoke at the 228th Anniversary of the Marine Corps, Nov, 2, 2003. With President George W. Bush.

Clockwise from top left: Crusade in Chung Ju, Korea; with Bill Bright in Moscow, Russia; with Bob Sorrell and Mark Dougharty in Panama; citywide crusade in Taipei, Taiwan; preaching in Spain with missionary son, David.

Clockwise from top left: Broadcasting around the world on "Love Worth Finding." With Billy Graham in 1950 (as a college student). In 1988 as president of the Southern Baptist Convention with Billy Graham. On the Board of "Focus On The Family" with James Dobson.

THE ROGERS' FAMILY CELEBRATING FIFTIETH WEDDING ANNIVERSARY, SEPT. 2, 2001

Left to right, front row—Jonathan, David (son), Kelly, and Stephen Rogers. *Back row left to right*—Michael, Adrian, Gayle (daughter), and Mike Foster, Adrian and Joyce. *Front row (right of middle)*—Andrew, Rachel, Angie (now Mrs. Nathan Luce) *Back row (right of middle)*—Janice (daughter) holding baby Breanna and Bryan Edmiston, Cindi, Steve (son) and *Seated far right*—Renae Rogers.

sat enthralled at his eloquence, conviction, and message content.

Dr. Lee is one of whom it could be said, "He is a legend in his own time." He was an icon in the field of preaching. Dr. Lee's preaching was bold with a cutting edge, yet he had a marvelous sense of humor and great charm. When he was scheduled to preach at the Southern Baptist Pastors' Conference program, I sat on the edge of my seat. (I'd arrived early to get an up-front seat.)

Little did I dream that one day I would pastor the Bellevue Church where Dr. Lee had pastored and *be* his pastor.

DR. W.A. CRISWELL, FORMER PASTOR, FIRST BAPTIST CHURCH, DALLAS

Dr. W.A. Criswell, whose ministry for many years paralleled that of Dr. Lee, was also a major influence. He was the renowned preacher and pastor of the great First Baptist Church of Dallas, Texas. He was highly educated (with an earned Ph.D.) and conversant in the biblical languages. However, he did not give scholarly dissertations, but rather impassioned and profound messages. He was scholarship on fire.

He was a featured speaker at national conventions and evangelism conferences. Crowds came to hear him, and he always hit a home run. As a boy, little did I dream I would one day preach a revival at the First Baptist Church of Dallas and be the featured speaker for Dr. Criswell's fortieth anniversary.

Dr. Criswell greatly influenced me because of his courageous stand for the inerrant Word of God. He was also an avowed premillenialist (as were all the other men already mentioned).

DR. B. GRAY ALLISON, PRESIDENT EMERITUS, MID-AMERICA BAPTIST THEOLOGICAL SEMINARY, MEMPHIS

Dr. B. Gray Allison was a brilliant young professor at New Orleans Seminary. I was in his class on missions and evangelism.

Dr. Allison had a passion for souls and a vision for missions like no other man I had ever met.

In the early days of the Southern Baptist controversy, Dr. Allison, who could have been an honored president of one of our six Southern Baptist Seminaries, chose to go against the tide and establish Mid-America Baptist Theological Seminary. Dr. Allison was put on the "non-approved" list of the denominational establishment quickly. While none of the other seminaries was willing to boldly stand for the inerrant Word of God, Dr. Allison founded a school on that belief. He was a driving force in the conservative resurgence.

I had the joy of inviting Dr. Allison to move the seminary from Little Rock, Ark., to Memphis when it was a fledgling school. They moved into a vacant Jewish Temple. The buildings were beautiful, and Dr. Allison called them "instant seminary." While the temple was being prepared, Mid-America Seminary met in the facilities of Bellevue Baptist Church.

Our church has been blessed by the influence of young seminarians in our midst. Dr. Allison yet today is a stalwart champion of the faith and continues to be a role model for me.

DR. VANCE HAVNER, EVANGELIST, BIBLE CONFERENCE SPEAKER

Dr. Vance Havner also impacted my life with his unique, penetrating, and practical messages. Dr. Havner was a master of the "turn of phrase" and epigrammatic style. Thousands of preachers (myself included) still quote Dr. Havner.

Sometimes I find myself asking, "How would Vance Havner say this?" He did not merely make a statement but he gave his words a barb that caused them to stick. It is impossible to forget Vance Havner once having heard or read him. My preaching has been colored by both the content and style of Vance Havner.

MAJOR W. IAN THOMAS, TORCHBEARERS OF THE CAPERNWRAY MISSIONARY FELLOWSHIP

Major Ian Thomas (referenced in chapter six) had a delightful, penetrating way of delivering truth. He was a guest in the church I pastored in Merritt Island and left an indelible mark on the congregation and my life.

His message on the all-sufficient Christ who indwells every believer continues to resonate in my heart and mind. He taught that every demand from God upon one's life is really a demand upon the Christ who lives within us.

He also taught the sufficiency of Christ in every situation. He verbalized the teaching in this way: "I can't; He never said I could. He can; He always said He would."

Major Thomas further impacted the Rogers' family for years to come. Our son Steve attended Major Thomas' Bible School in Capernwray, England, and was influenced by his teaching.

DR. STEPHEN F. OLFORD, OLFORD MINISTRIES INTERNATIONAL

A spiritual giant whom I admired and from whom I learned was Stephen F. Olford. He was born of missionary parents in Africa and became a world-renowned preacher, pastor, and evangelist. He was often called "a preacher's preacher" and "the prince of preachers." In his last years he gave himself to teaching principles of preaching at the Stephen F. Olford Institute for Biblical Preaching. People came from around the world to attend these sessions.

I was enamored with Dr. Olford's ability to quote and crack open biblical texts with fresh insight and homiletic skill. I was thrilled when he moved his Institute for Biblical Preaching to Memphis and when he and Mrs. Olford placed their membership at Bellevue Baptist Church. I enjoyed many hours of rich fellowship with them. Also, I was honored to deliver the message at Dr. Olford's memorial service after his homegoing in September 2004.

DR. J. SIDLOW BAXTER, BIBLE TEACHER, AUTHOR

I first heard J. Sidlow Baxter in Daytona Beach, Fla. He spoke at the Pastor's Conference of the Florida Baptist Convention in the 1960s. His

British accent, wit, impeccable speech, and theological content stirred me. I remember the content of that first sermon.

I made it a point to meet Dr. Baxter after the service. He was an elegant man in appearance. I sometimes thought, *He has a head start on most preachers because he even looks holy!*

Dr. Baxter wrote a book titled, *A Strategic Grasp of the Scripture*. He modeled the content of that book. Dr. Baxter ministered at Bellevue on various occasions and was greatly loved by the congregation.

Before coming to America, he was pastor in Edinburgh, Scotland. Dr. Baxter could charm almost anyone with statements like "Am I boring you? Say no!" I still read from his writings.

DR. BILL BRIGHT, CAMPUS CRUSADE FOR CHRIST

A man who stretched my vision perhaps more than any man was Dr. Bill Bright. He may have been a greater driving force in fulfilling the great commission than any other man in this century. He, with his wife, Vonette, founded Campus Crusade for Christ, a dynamic ministry that began on college campuses and circled the globe with thousands of workers.

Every time I thought I was thinking big and then met with Bill Bright, I came away feeling like a pigmy. Dr. Bright's eyes would glow as he talked about fulfilling the Great Commission in our generation.

He and I were close friends, and as mentioned earlier on one occasion we ministered together in Red Square in Moscow preaching the gospel during the Orthodox Easter season. What an experience that was. Thousands listened in person, and the program was telecast nationwide on state television. I would never have dreamed such a thing was possible, but Bill Bright was a dreamer of great dreams and a seer of great visions.

He led out in conferences on prayer and fasting, and it has been my privilege to attend all of them. He showed me that our God is a mighty God and is able to do exploits.

I visited with him a few days before his death. He was still challenging me to attempt greater things in the name of Jesus. I was blessed to be able to speak at his memorial service in Orlando. His life continues to impact millions.

Of course there are others who have touched Adrian's life along with these. Adrian says his ministry and preaching are mosaics of bits and pieces these dear men, and many others like them, have placed in his life.

CHAPTER

17

WHAT OTHERS
HAVE SAID

Just as Adrian's ministry has been impacted by many other men of God, so too his ministry has had a powerful impact upon the callings of fellow believers on their journeys of faith and ministry.

On the following pages, we've given some of these friends, confidantes, family members, colleagues, and congregation members the opportunity to offer their perspectives on what Adrian means to them.

Lifetime Friends

DR. JOE BOATWRIGHT, PASTOR EMERITUS, ALOMA BAPTIST CHURCH, WINTER PARK, FLA.

What a journey we have been on together. We thank God that, in His plan, we met so early in our ministry. You have both had great influences on our lives these almost fifty years.

Your love for the Lord Jesus and the Word of God has motivated us to keep that the first priority in our own lives. You have blessed us as we have been eyewitnesses to your family relationships and your love for each other.

Your friendship has been, and is, one of our great joys in life. Through all the years, you have been associated with so many wonderful and even great people and in spite of this, you have kept us as one of the five fingers on which, as you've said, we count our true friends. We love you and thank God for your lives.

REV. PETER LORD, PASTOR EMERITUS, PARK AVENUE BAPTIST CHURCH, TITUSVILLE, FLA.

It has been a long time since we met at seminary. The Monopoly™ games and bull sessions were good. We remember all the years when we were close in Brevard county.

All the times we shared together. The camping. The churches growing and we also as persons. The times in the Winnebago camper in Colorado and other places. The time we went to Jamaica together. The time on vacation when you called and asked us to pray with you about going to Bellevue—a decision we were both glad and sad about (glad for you and the church, sad because you were leaving).

DR. JEFF STILES, MINISTER TO SENIOR ADULTS, GREEN RIVER BAPTIST CHURCH, WAYNESBORO, TENN.

Words cannot adequately express what your friendship has meant to me all of these years. I suppose of our fifty years in the ministry Louise and I have known you two for forty-eight of them.

From those days as young married college kids living in the same trailer park until the present, your consistent lives of faithfulness to the Lord have had a great impact on us.

DR. HAROLD O'CHESTER, PASTOR EMERITUS, GREAT HILLS BAPTIST CHURCH, AUSTIN, TEXAS

When we were in seminary, we usually met in the coffee shop several times a week, but on Friday it was different. Most Fridays, Adrian would come to the coffee shop with his books and the mail he would have just picked up. In his mail would be a weekly periodical which presented the best evangelical sermons of the past 100 years. I watched often as Adrian would read the sermon through and then begin to outline it in alliterative language, better than the author.

Thirty-four years ago I began to have a daily quiet time with the Lord. Adrian is one of the men I have prayed for every day—that God would use him beyond his wildest dreams. He has!

WAYNE ALLEN, FORMER PASTOR, BRIARWOOD BAPTIST CHURCH, CORDOVA, TENN.

Adrian Rogers is the absolute example of what it means to be a man of integrity. In our friendship of over 30 years, Adrian has been and continues to be an encourager to me. We have been faithful prayer partners through times of joy and heartache. Whether on vacation together or in a restaurant, with our families or just the two of us, at conventions or in church, Adrian always manifests the spirit and image of Jesus Christ. God has used Adrian to open many doors of ministry for me. In our relationship he has always proven what a true friend is.

Southern Baptist Convention Peers

DR. PAIGE PATTERSON, PRESIDENT, SOUTHWESTERN BAPTIST THEOLOGICAL SEMINARY

Only a few times in any century does a man rise out of the ranks of the ordinary with a touch of God upon him in such a way as to change the course of all human history.

Further, it is extraordinary that that man be a man of impeccable moral standards, possessing a pastor's heart, remarkable alacrity, profound dedication to the work of the Savior, and pulpit eloquence and brilliance unmatched by others.

To say that is exactly what God gave the world in Adrian Rogers is not an attempt to fell the oak of your humility, but only to recognize what most of us know is true in order to praise God for what He has done through you, and to thank you for allowing God to have the use of all your talents and abilities.

DR. ROBERT RECCORD, PRESIDENT, NORTH AMERICAN MISSION BOARD, SOUTHERN BAPTIST CONVENTION

I cannot begin to imagine the number of lives you have touched, not only in America, but also around the world. I know beyond question that I am one of those lives. Though I will never know the price you paid, I must say how thankful I am that you were our standard bearer in the conservative resurgence.

Your leadership gave us bearing in the rough seas of change. For that, I will always be thankful. Thanks for getting out of your comfort zone and granting the leadership that was desperately needed to bring us back to our historic roots.

DR. BAILEY SMITH, EVANGELIST, BAILEY SMITH MINISTRIES, ATLANTA, GA.

I have known you as a co-worker in our denomination and have the conviction that you are the best thing that ever happened to the conservative resurgence.

Your ability to preach, your integrity, and your commanding presence were an anchor for this great ship destined for the shores of revival. Only eternity will be able to measure your contribution to the Southern Baptist Convention.

DR. JAMES T. DRAPER, JR., PRESIDENT, LIFEWAY CHRISTIAN RESOURCES

I know of no one who has been more significant in the life of Southern Baptists and the evangelical community than you have been and continue to be.

God has blessed you with a unique ability to proclaim His Word; and you do it with power, creativity, and passion. I am deeply grateful for all you have meant to Carol Ann and me.

DR. MORRIS CHAPMAN, PRESIDENT AND CHIEF OFFICER, EXECUTIVE COMMITTEE OF THE SOUTHERN BAPTIST CONVENTION

Along with thousands, both laity and ministers, who have been touched by your life and ministry, I am grateful you answered the call of God to preach the gospel. God has honored your unwavering faithfulness by sending you forth to preach to the uttermost part of the earth.

Both your life and your preaching have been a testimony to untold numbers of younger preachers, who have seen Christ in you and heard a word from the Lord through a voice that in itself is a special gift from the Lord. All who know you, even those who disagreed with your convictions, admire you as a man after God's own heart.

DR. B. GRAY ALLISON, PRESIDENT EMERITUS, MID-AMERICA BAPTIST THEOLOGICAL SEMINARY

As I think of your fifty years of ministry, I am most thankful to God for your faithfulness to Him and to His Word. I have never seen you waver in that faithfulness.

Thank you for your friendship and help for Mid-America Baptist Theological Seminary during the twenty-nine years of her existence. You were our friend when we had few friends. I thank God that you never wavered in that friendship.

DR. JACK GRAHAM, PASTOR, PRESTONWOOD BAPTIST CHURCH, PLANO, TEXAS

I want to express my deep love, admiration, and appreciation for you. I think you know how much you are loved across our denominational world, and indeed, our evangelical faith.

My ministry has been impacted in scores of positive ways because of your influence. I love you and thank God for the privilege of being your friend.

DR. CHARLES F. STANLEY, PASTOR, FIRST BAPTIST CHURCH, ATLANTA; SPEAKER, IN TOUCH MINISTRIES

I praise God for your faithfulness to share the Word of God and shepherd your flock. So many have received abundantly from you, but the most blessed thought of all is that our Lord will never forget your labor of love.

DR. JERRY VINES, PASTOR, FIRST BAPTIST CHURCH, JACKSONVILLE, FLA.

Adrian, although I didn't get to hear you preach fifty years ago, I have heard you these thirty plus years now. Every time I have heard you preach, you helped me love the Lord Jesus more and gave me a desire to live for Him and serve Him more effectively. Thank you, dear friend, for every blessing I have received from your preaching ministry.

DR. H. EDWIN YOUNG, PASTOR, SECOND BAPTIST CHURCH, HOUSTON, TEXAS

You are a model of pastoral leadership for all who have followed your ministry through the years. Your stance on the inerrancy of God's Word has never wavered, and your courage in the pulpit has been a constant reminder of how a pastor should rightly divide the Word of God.

DR. JERRY FALWELL, PASTOR, THOMAS ROAD BAPTIST CHURCH, LYNCHBURG, VA.; CHANCELLOR, LIBERTY UNIVERSITY

Your life has touched millions of people around the world. I consider you one of God's giants and a true hero of our times. You have been used by Him to build one of the greatest churches, evangelize Memphis, reach Tennessee, turn the Southern Baptist Convention, and impact the world for Christ. This is a life's work in itself, but I believe your greatest days are still ahead.

DR. JAMES MERRITT, PASTOR, CROSS POINTE CHURCH, DULUTH, GA.

What a legacy you will take with you to heaven—fifty years and more of faithfully preaching the gospel, modeling what a man of God should be, as well as being one of the key leaders in turning the largest denomination in history back to her biblical roots. Dr. Rogers, I send this letter with my unqualified and absolute admiration and respect for all you have done for the cause of Christ.

I wish words could tell you how much you mean to me—perhaps in eternity, before the Lord Jesus, I can tell you again how much you have meant to my life.

I assure you there has never been a younger preacher who loves and respects you more than I do. I can also tell you that you have never had a greater impact on any man than on me.

DR. STEVE GAINES, PASTOR, FIRST BAPTIST CHURCH, GARDENDALE, ALA.

Thank you for the friendship you have extended toward me over the years. Thank you for allowing me to preach to your people. I consider you to be one of the greatest mentors God has ever placed in my life.

You have been a Paul to me, and it has been my privilege to be one of your many Timothys.

Thank you for being so bold in your convictions and so steadfast in your integrity and faithfulness. Thank you for helping lead our Southern Baptist Convention back to a place of theological conservatism. Thank you also for being America's pastor through your television ministry.

Other Religious Leaders

MAJOR IAN THOMAS, TORCHBEARERS OF THE CAPERNWRAY MISSIONARY FELLOWSHIP

Adrian, you are one of the few who has had courage enough to remain true to the Lord Jesus and to the gospel as He proclaimed it, in all its fullness and divine simplicity. We thank God for you.

DR. J. SIDLOW BAXTER, AUTHOR, BIBLE TEACHER.

You are one of God's most powerful prophet-voices to present-day America.

Over hills and dales, in every direction your Spirit-anointed and televised ministry propagates gospel truth and Bible doctrine. Many thousands listen to the Word of the Lord through you, to the saving of their souls and the enriching of their lives.

DR. BILLY GRAHAM, BILLY GRAHAM EVANGELISTIC ASSOCIATION

You have my deepest admiration for how true and faithful you have been to the Scriptures. In describing you today, I expect many others will use the term "prince of preachers," because that is a title you have justly earned.

You have held the highest offices in the Southern Baptist Convention, and yet you have continued to find the time for so many other ministries. There is no way to tell, this side of heaven, how many people the Lord has touched through your "Love Worth Finding" television and radio ministry across America. Your books and preaching ministry have extended your outreach around the world. You have one of the biggest churches in the country, and yet I am told it has the atmosphere of a small church.

Others far more eloquent than I will express their appreciation to you for all you have meant to the Kingdom of God. I just want to say I am personally honored to call you my friend.

GEORGE BEVERLY SHEA, SOLOIST, BILLY GRAHAM EVANGELISTIC ASSOCIATION

What a delight to be associated with you in the beautiful pictorial book, *The Wonder of It All*—with precious comments from your heart and pen. Your friendship—your ministry—so much appreciated.

DR. STEPHEN F. OLFORD, OLFORD MINISTRIES INTERNATIONAL

Your ministry from the pulpit, on radio, and around the world is heaven's endorsement of your evangelical stand, evangelistic spirit, and expository style. No one can dispute the fact that God honors the preaching of His Word in the power of the Holy Spirit—even in a postmodern age of rationalistic relativism and pluralistic syncretism.

BILL GAITHER, GOSPEL SONG WRITER, GAITHER FAMILY RESOURCES

You are dear friends whom we don't see enough. We love you and thank God for you.

DR. BILL BRIGHT, CAMPUS CRUSADE FOR CHRIST, ORLANDO, FLA.

You have been a godly role model, challenging many to passionately pursue the Lord's plan for their lives. At a time in our history when many Christian leaders are falling away from the faith or are succumbing to the pressures of this world, it is inspiring to see your marvelous example as a true statesman of Christ. Your close friendship these past forty years in particular has been an invaluable source of joy and comfort to me.

DR. JAMES C. DOBSON, CHAIRMAN, FOCUS ON THE FAMILY

I consider it a privilege to offer a few words about Dr. Adrian Rogers, whom I count among my most trusted and respected friends. In addition to heading one of the busiest and most influential ministries in the United States, Adrian has earned the love, admiration and high esteem of millions of people.

His friends at Focus are well aware that his service on our Board has come at a personal sacrifice, and we owe him a debt of gratitude for lending us his talent and vision.

The Board has been strengthened and bolstered by his presence—we've all come to rely on his great store of wisdom and insight.

Shirley and I have such love and appreciation for Adrian and Joyce—not for what they've accomplished, but for who they are.

They consistently and faithfully align their lives with the principles of God's Word, and it's abundantly evident that they love Jesus Christ with every fiber of their being.

CHUCK COLSON, CHAIRMAN, PRISON FELLOWSHIP

You are one of the great, towering figures of our time. Over the years you've been a wonderful model to me, and I have appreciated your friendship and Joyce's, which goes back to the earliest days of the ministry. In my opinion you are one of the truly great preachers in America today and a beloved friend. You are God's man with God's message.

LETTER TO THE EDITOR, *COMMERCIAL APPEAL*, DECEMBER 16, 2004

BLESSED BY A SPIRITUAL GIANT

Thank you for your excellent article on Dr. Adrian Rogers, as he prepares to retire as senior minister of Bellevue Baptist Church ("A big opening to fill/With Rev. Adrian Rogers turning over the reins, Bellevue

Baptist needs another God-sent man," Nov. 28).

We have loved him as a brother and have been mentored by him. We thank God for bringing him to Memphis. Dr. Rogers has an incredible, God-anointed ability to proclaim the gospel. He is a spiritual giant whose influence reaches across denominational, cultural, and national boundaries.

As his prayer partners, our prayer is that his influence on behalf of Christ will continue to be felt for many years to come. He is finishing well, which we all desire to do.

SENIOR MINISTRIES:
BILL BOUKNIGHT, CHRIST UNITED METHODIST CHURCH
HOWARD CLARK, FIRST EVANGELICAL CHURCH
SAM SHAW, GERMANTOWN BAPTIST CHURCH
JOHN SARTELLE, INDEPENDENT PRESBYTERIAN CHURCH
SANDERS WILLSON, SECOND PRESBYTERIAN CHURCH

National and State Leaders

GEORGE W. BUSH, PRESIDENT OF THE UNITED STATES OF AMERICA

A strong spiritual foundation is central to the lives of Americans. By sharing God's teachings with your congregation, you have enriched the lives of countless individuals and served as an inspiration to the community. Our nation is a better place because of your dedication to sharing your wisdom, guidance, and faith with others.

GEORGE H. W. BUSH, FORMER PRESIDENT OF THE UNITED STATES OF AMERICA

Here is a man whom Southern Baptists have kept coming to. He served them earlier as president of the Convention and now again.

On top of everything else, he pastors one of the largest churches in the world. ... There are many who presume to speak for the evangelical movement, but surely Dr. Rogers is one of the handful who truly represent them. Here is a great man with a lot of influence and a lot of wisdom.

JIMMY CARTER, FORMER PRESIDENT OF THE UNITED STATES OF AMERICA

Since meeting with you at The Carter Center, I have thought about you often, and continue to respect the enormous influence you have in the Christian community. I have never forgotten that we prayed together for guidance in how the divisions among Baptists might be healed. With faith in answered prayer, we cannot afford to overlook any opportunities to heal "the tensions in the southern Baptist Convention." Please let me know whenever you have any ideas.

WILLIAM H. FRIST, M.D., MAJORITY LEADER, UNITED STATES SENATE

Dr. Rogers is truly an outstanding citizen. As the pastor of one of the largest churches in America, Dr. Rogers is a positive influence on the 29,000 members of his congregation and many others in the Memphis community.

Dr. Rogers' inspirational message reaches far beyond the borders of Tennessee. He is heard daily on radio and television, and his international ministry, "Love Worth Finding," has brought hope and encouragement to many who are hurting and struggling with serious life decisions.

SURDEN ENGLAND, SECRETARY OF THE NAVY

It was simply delightful and inspiring to hear you speak at the United States Marine Corp Worship Service at the National Cathedral. It was also most gracious of you and Joyce to give your weekend to the Marines.

We are indeed a nation under God, and that is our heritage and our future. May God bless you for all you do for America and for keeping the flame of faith burning for all peoples.

DON SUNDQUIST, FORMER GOVERNOR, TENNESSEE

I wanted to let you know how grateful I am for your being with us during the inaugural festivities. Martha and I enjoyed your inspiring participation in the official ceremony. Thank you for your friendship and for the generosity of your time and talent.

Some of the Bellevue Staff

DR. JAMES D. WHITMIRE, MINISTER OF MUSIC

I have known Adrian Rogers for forty-one years. I have worked with him for thirty-eight of those years. If I could encapsulate the man and his ministry in one sentence, I would say, "He is a man of his word."

This sentence has a two-fold meaning. First, he is a man of His Word; he loves God, loves the Word of God, believes the Word of God, and lives the Word of God. Second, he is a man of his own word: he keeps his vows and his word to his wife and family, to his staff and church, to his friends and creditors, and to his Lord. I have seen him in all kinds of situations (sad, glad, and mad) for forty-one years, and I know he lives what he preaches.

He is quick to apologize to others and quick to confess his sin to the Lord. He does not preach one thing from the pulpit and live another way when he is out of the pulpit. He is consistent. He genuinely wants to stay clean before the Lord. This makes for the wonderful Holy Spirit power in his life and preaching ministry.

After my parents and my wife Linda, Adrian Rogers has had the most profound influence in my life. He taught me as a young minister of music to love the Bible as the Word of God, infallible and perfect without error; to love Jesus, God's Son and sacrificial Lamb; to love the Cross and to know without a doubt that my sin debt was paid by the shedding of Jesus' blood; to love my wife, second only to Jesus.

God was so good to my wife and me to link our life's ministry with Adrian and Joyce Rogers. Our lives and our children's lives have been changed through his preaching from the pulpit and his preaching by the example of a life well lived for Jesus (Phil. 1:3-6).

REV. ROBERT L. SORRELL, FORMER ASSOCIATE PASTOR; FOUNDER, *THE ASSOCIATE*

Your faithfulness to our Lord is an inspiration to me. Your friendship is and has been one of my most prized possessions. The fruit of your life and ministry has been abundant and without question. You will always be a producer, but the season of ripening is a blessed time for the one who has faithfully tilled the vineyard.

Rev. Mark Dougharty, associate pastor

Words cannot express what you have meant to me from the first time I heard you speak on a Sunday evening until this hour. You have had a profound impact on my life. Much of what I know about theology and application of the Scriptures I have learned from you. You have been my example for wisdom, caution, personal holiness, and leadership.

Linda Glance, administrative assistant to the pastor

I want to say a special thanks to you for the privilege of serving with you these thirty-two years. First, thank you for having a high standard of excellence. I have been challenged to achieve more and to adopt an "I can" attitude.

Second, thank you for the incredible work experience you gave me. When I think of the thousands of sermon outlines, letters, manuscripts, and memos I have typed, the innumerable phone calls I have handled, the travel I have arranged, the many ministry opportunities and so much more, it has been a rich experience.

Finally, I express my heartfelt thanks to you for being a godly example, for your encouragement to focus on and be faithful to the Lord Jesus Christ, and your challenge to believe, trust and obey the Word of God. Sunday after Sunday, year after year, you have preached the Word and have lifted up the name of Jesus. Your love for Him and devotion to Him cause me to want to know, love, and serve Him in a greater way. "May the Lord reward you for what you have done" (Ruth 2:12, HCSB).

A Few of the Preachers Called Under Adrian Rogers' Ministry

Dr. Ken Whitten, pastor, Idlewild Baptist Church, Tampa, Fla.

Pastor, I never realized how much I knew about ministry until I left Bellevue. I studied right so often, that wrong became so obvious. Thank you for believing in me, investing in me, and fathering me in the ministry. So much of who I am is Jesus through you.

Dr. David H. McKinley, teaching pastor, Prestonwood Baptist Church, Plano, Texas

Through your contagious smile and courageous preaching, my life has been touched, challenged, and blessed. Thank you for modeling steadfastness and fruitfulness.

Thank you for demonstrating courage and conviction. Thank you for being true to the Bible and for loving Jesus.

Rev. Glenn Rogers, director of evangelism and prayer, Nevada Baptist Convention

Thank you for being faithful to Jesus and the gospel, no tangents, just the truth that makes a difference for all eternity. Thank you for faithfulness to your family, which is such a great example. Thank you, also, for being a faithful friend. The unconditional love you show to us and many others is redemptive, encouraging, and full of grace and mercy.

Rev. Greg Addison, pastor, Eastside Baptist Church, Paragould, Ark.

Words cannot adequately explain how much I love you both as a minister and as a man. Your ministry has been an integral part of my life. You ordained me as a deacon at twenty-seven, and ordained me as a preacher of the gospel of Jesus Christ at thirty-one.

My theological training was in your sanctuary, and my ministry training as part of your staff. The Apostle Paul spoke of Timothy as a ministry son; I will always know you as my ministry father.

Thank you for teaching me the Word of God and for teaching me to love the Word of God. Thank you for being faithful to our Savior and to His Word.

A Few of the Missionaries Called Under Adrian Rogers' Ministry

DAVID BLEDSOE, BELO HORIZONTE, BRAZIL

As members out of Bellevue, we saw God use your leadership to move us toward fellowship with Him, witnessing for Him, and now planting churches in another area of the world.

ALAN DUNCAN, PORT ELIZABETH, SOUTH AFRICA

You may not remember this old Memphis Showboat place kicker, but we count with great joy the years Andrea and I sat under your ministry at Bellevue.

God used your powerful exposition of the Word to challenge us to follow Him wherever He leads and to know that He is fully trustworthy. God bless you for being faithful where God planted you and for having a heart for Jesus that has touched the world.

The first television message I saw preached in South Africa almost nine years ago was a "Love Worth Finding" video of you preaching the unsearchable riches of Christ. I told my African friends proudly, "Dr. Rogers was my pastor."

DR. ROBIN HADAWAY, REGIONAL LEADER, SOUTH AMERICA, INTERNATIONAL MISSION BOARD, SOUTHERN BAPTIST CONVENTION

We have served since 1984 with the International Mission Board in Tanzania, Kenya, Sudan, and Brazil. Dr. Rogers not only was an inspiration to enter the ministry, but he continues to be a mentor, a model, and a friend. Dr. and Mrs. Rogers exemplify the Christian family and provide the biblical inspiration for us to continue in ministry and reach out to the ends of the earth.

KEITH MOORE, CHURCH PLANTER, TEGUCIGALPA, HONDURAS

Your life and example have been great blessings to Dawn and me. We have learned from you to walk closer to the Lord and have been challenged to a higher call. The Lord used you in a great way to confirm in both of us His desire for us to serve Him full-time overseas in church-planting.

A Few of the Many Church Members of All Ages

LEAH HICKMAN, AGE NINE, CHILDREN'S DEPARTMENT

I'll miss you when you retire. There will never be a greater pastor. I love you and your preaching. We were there the day you told us. We also saw it on the news. I really wish [for]at least another year. Some of the hymns we sang Sunday were my favorite too. I hope you have a great retired life.

BETSY McKINLEY, AGE NINE, CHILDREN'S DEPARTMENT

Do not let Dr. Rogers retire: because I love him like a father, and he is my preacher! I love you very much!

DARBY THOMPSON, AGE EIGHT, CHILDREN'S DEPARTMENT

Dear Dr. and Mrs. Rogers, I love you so much. Thank you for teaching my family about God. I love being in Mrs. Rogers' class. I will really miss you very much. I am glad that you and Mrs. Rogers teach me about God. Thank you for teaching the church. I love to go to church and see you preach at church. I love learning about God.

KAITLIN ALLEN, AGE FIFTEEN, BELLEVUE YOUTH DIVISION

My hero is Dr. Adrian Rogers. He is my pastor. I think he is a good Christian. He's kind of funny. My parents love him. He works at Bellevue Church. Bellevue Church is huge. It's easy to get lost in there.

I really like him.

TIFFANY KNIGHT, AGE FOURTEEN, BELLEVUE YOUTH DIVISION

When I first heard about your retirement I was devastated. I looked back on all the years I've spent at this church hearing one voice: yours.

I am only fourteen years old. I was baptized here, saved within the foundations of this church and praised and worshipped since 1995 in the church.

From the time I stepped foot in the building and was old enough to understand, you changed my life through your teachings of God. You made me see that someone as young as myself can make a change for the better.

I am one to stand up for what I believe in, and every Sunday you send me home with a message.

I am only one of thousands of people who attend this church, but I want you to know how much you have impacted my life.

You are my hero.

J. ROBERT VINCENT, M.D., DEACON

It seems just yesterday that I first sat in your Pastor's Discovery Class. Since that day I have been sitting at your feet soaking up God's Word. You changed my life. As a result of your teaching, I have tried to become more like you and Christ each and every day. Maybe—someday.

Barbara and I have enjoyed working with the youth on the mission trips. We have seen these young people when they are "for real." You would not be able to see them the way they really are because they would be on their best behavior with you.

We have seen how growing up under your ministry, they have not only received Christ as their Savior, but have made Him Lord of their lives. They are totally committed.

It is hard to say in words how much you mean to me. All I know is that God had a purpose in sending you into my life. I thank Him every day, and I thank you.

JOSH MANNING, AGE NINETEEN
"THE EMBODIMENT OF INTEGRITY" (EXCERPT FROM AN ESSAY FOR ENGLISH CLASS)

In a day when men sway with the slightest breeze, fall to the smallest temptations, and acquiesce to the least pressure, I find myself asking, "Are there any men of integrity left, and, if so, will they endure into the next generation?" Surely if they do not carry on, the world will diminish, leaving men in a more dismal state of affairs than we have seen heretofore. I shudder at the thought of this fate. There is no question that without men of integrity and honor our society not only *will* cease to exist. It *must*.

The answer to the problem posed by the moral weakness that permeates every part of our society is to instill in the upcoming generation a sense of integrity, a sense of goodness, and perhaps even a sense of righteousness.

I know a man who is working toward that end. He is a personal friend and hero. He possesses great meekness, greater wisdom, and a grand measure of integrity. The one to whom I am referring is my pastor, Dr. Adrian Rogers; the qualities I have mentioned are not individual and separate from each other in his character.

They blend in his being to form an incredible man whom I would recommend without stutter, stammer, apology, or equivocation as a role model for any young person today. Dr. Rogers' vibrant personality and warm manner lends an amiability that is possessed by him and well exercised by even fewer. Using his joviality combined with an iron clad moral compass, he directs tens of thousands to live a godly lifestyle every week.

Dr. Rogers is what he is. His yea means yea, and his nay means nay. He makes no apology for declaring the truth, and he holds an unwavering belief in absolute right and wrong. The dangers of moral relativism and situational ethics are dealt a severe blow by his well-thought-out arguments, persuasive examples, and prodigious knowledge of Scripture. Having the blessing of knowing him personally allows me to state authoritatively that he is the same in the pulpit and out, at church or home, in his office or on the lake. ...

Adrian Rogers is a beacon of light to a world in which the shadows lengthen; he is a bold voice crying, "There is an answer, and His name is Jesus"; a man who lives what he preaches.

Loving Tributes from the Rogers Children

Thank you, Dad, for investing in my future. Thank you for helping me see what things are really important. Thank you for challenging me through the years to be a people person and a leader. Thank you for being a role model for all your children. Thank you for living out in private the same things you preach in public.

Thank you and Mom for being our silent partners in ministry and life throughout the years, and especially recently as Cindi, Renae and I are charting new waters.

Thank you for your unyielding love for the truth and your unwavering love for Jesus. I'm glad you're my Dad!

WITH LOVE AND AFFECTION, YOUR SON STEVE

How would it be possible to tell the things I admire about my father, much less adequately express my love for him? I could not even begin. But I will tell you there are three things that make him the great man and even greater father that he is.

First is his consistency. I know of few children who could say they have never, a single time heard their father curse, lie, gossip, or belittle someone else. What my father is in the pulpit, he is in the home when no one is looking.

Second is his wisdom. My father always knows best. He thinks from God's point of view and can be counted on not just to give an acceptable answer, but to know what to do, how to do it, when to do it, and why to do it. He has the discernment that makes him not just a great speaker and preacher, but more importantly a great man, a great leader, and a great father.

Finally, I admire his convictions. He stands for the truth when it is unpopular, inconvenient, and not politically correct. Growing up, I was frustrated many times by not being able to do the things everyone else was doing.

Looking back, I can see I have been blessed beyond measure by being able to sit under his preaching of the infallible Word of God. I have been doubly blessed to have seen that infallible Word of God lived out in the life of a great and godly man.

I LOVE YOU, GAYLE

Dear Daddy:

We, alongside many others who have spent time under your ministry, have greatly benefited down through the years from a steady diet of sound biblical teaching and Spirit-filled preaching. We have been impacted by your deep commitment to a vision for seeing souls saved, growing a healthy church, and above all, glorifying God.

But besides all this, we, unlike others, have been able to know you not only in the limelight, but also behind the scenes in the intimacy of family life. We have had the opportunity to see close-up the living sermons of flesh and blood behind the words proclaimed publicly. And we have never felt disappointed or defrauded.

Besides the grace of God in my life, I owe what I am, more than anything else, to you, who, as godly parents, loved me through thick and thin, brought me up in the nurture and admonition of the Lord, knew how to recognize and ask forgiveness for your shortcomings, and showed me in your daily example what it means to love the Lord with all one's heart, soul, and mind.

I LOVE YOU, DAVID

Dear Daddy:

As you know, my tears have been flowing freely today because of my deep sorrow over your resignation. However, my joy abounds, because I can hold my head up high to know that you have walked faithfully your whole ministry. I am so proud of you.

These have been the "The Glory Years." I have been privileged to experience unbelievable events—i.e. the momentous swing back to conservatism of the Southern Baptist Convention, "Claiming Our Canaan" etc. It's hard to realize that I have been a part of history in the making.

But more important to me is that I get to have you as my Daddy. Why me, when so many others would long to hold that coveted position?

Thanks for "running the race" in such a way as to give me a major head start. I promise to carry the baton in a way that would not dishonor you and Mom, and to pass it on to our children. Truly, "The generation of the upright shall be blessed" (Ps. 112:2).

WITH ALL MY LOVE, JANICE

PART TWO
THE PREACHING PHILOSOPHY
OF ADRIAN ROGERS

Researched by Dennis Brunet

CHAPTER

18

HOMILETICAL PHILOSOPHY

Part two of this book is an examination of the ministry philosophy of Adrian Rogers. The researcher, Dennis Brunet, explored the following five areas that were instrumental in shaping Adrian Rogers' homiletical philosophy: the dynamic of the Spirit of God; the dynamic of the Word of God; the dynamic of the man of God; the dynamic of the house of God; and the dynamic of preaching the Word of God.

Q. Discuss the preacher's dependence upon the Spirit of God.

The preacher can produce no lasting work apart from total dependence and submission to the Holy Spirit. Only the Holy Spirit can cause men to understand and believe the gospel. I may *preach* truth, but only the Holy Spirit can impart truth.

It takes more than the power of persuasion to be a good preacher. The preacher is completely dependent upon the work of the Holy Spirit for power in the ministry. Not only is Jesus the person of truth, the Holy Spirit is the power of truth.

Q. Discuss the work of the Holy Spirit in preaching.

Following my response to God's call to enter the gospel ministry, I had an experience with the Holy Spirit that occurred during my senior year of high school.

I had a burden to be used of God. I often walked alone on the football field to pray: When I was a kid preacher and God called me to preach, I was a football player down in West Palm Beach, Fla. The football practice field was near our house. I remember going out there on many a summer night in Florida, honored, awed that God would call me to preach. I would walk up and down that football field and say, "Thank You, Lord, for calling me to preach."

My frequent prayer was, "Oh God, I want You to use me."

I would describe myself as theologically ignorant concerning the ministry of the Holy Spirit. At the time of my experience, I had no Bible background. I could not have told you from Bible chronology who came first, Abraham or Moses. About all I knew concerning the Holy Spirit was that God was three in one—Father, Son, and Holy Spirit—and that the church baptized with The Trinitarian Formula.

Despite my limited understanding, I desired to commit my life completely to God.

One night, walking on the football field, I felt a need to kneel and pray. Alone on that football field, I called out to the Lord, "God, I want You to use me!" Kneeling did not seem good enough or humble enough, so I laid down prostrate in the grass and said, "Father, I want You to use me." That did not seem humble enough, so I took my finger and made a hole in the dirt and put my nose down in that hole. I called out, "Lord, I am as low as I know how to get. I want You to use me."

The Holy Spirit is sovereign and His work is dynamic, creative, and demands a naiveté on the part of God's servants. Something happened in my life that night. I didn't have ecstasies or a vision of any kind, but there was a transformation. Although I did not understand the theology concerning the Holy Spirit, there was a deeper commitment to Christ, and I believe I had a personal experience with the Holy Spirit and was filled with the Spirit that night.

My early sermons were poor, both in structure and form. The Holy Spirit, however, gave life and energy to the truth that was preached. I would be less than honest to deny that God graciously released His power into my young heart and life.

The truth of the Word of God was made powerful because the anointing of the Holy Spirit was upon my preaching. God's hand was on my ministry. I know that now by remembrance and hindsight after having seen the Holy Spirit work these many years. God was working supernaturally in the life of a teenage preacher.

Q. What is the difference between anointing and unction?

I believe a preacher should never enter the pulpit without the anointing of the Holy Spirit. I had rather die than to preach without the anointing of the Holy Spirit of God.

The concept of anointing is difficult to define and has sometimes been erroneously confused with conviction, passion, or personal gifts. I would define *anointing* as a quickening, an empowering, an enlightening, a boldness, or an insight that the Holy Spirit imparts to the preacher. The inability to differentiate between anointing and soulish preaching has prevented many preachers from being successful in the ministry.

I view as vital the preacher's ability to distinguish between soulish preaching and Holy Spirit-anointed preaching. Many times a preacher will wrongly assume that he has preached with anointing, because soulish preaching at first appears to be powerful and effective. There are many times when a preacher may think that he is preaching with anointing when he is not. Many times, a man will step down from the pulpit and say, "I really did it this morning. I was good! I really preached with Holy Ghost power," and, in reality, he did not.

By rejecting soulish preaching, I am not rejecting the preacher's personality. When I say that soulish preaching is bad, I do not mean the human soul is bad.

In my theology, I am a trichotomist; that is, I believe that man is body, soul, and spirit. The human soul is comprised by man's mind, emotion, and will. Soul is that which makes you, you and me, me. Soul is good when it is subjected to the Holy Spirit. All good preaching has soul in it, for preaching is truth through human personality.

The true test of whether a preacher is proclaiming God's Word through the power of soulish preaching or through the anointing of the Spirit is: Does the message cause fruit to remain? When a man is preaching in the Spirit, God is doing a work. His work lasts for eternity, and God is glorified because he bears fruit in the ministry. Soulish preaching does not cause fruit to remain because man is preaching outside the anointing of God's Spirit.

The soulish preacher is attempting to persuade through human reason. This type of preaching may entertain, it may inform, but it will not endure, nor will it ultimately change the individual.

I see the word *unction* used in a slightly different sense. When a man is set aside for God's work and filled with the Spirit, he has "unction from the Holy One." That is, he has been selected and gifted to serve. Yet when a man has unction and the Spirit of God is within him, he would still need anointing, which is a special touch for a specific task.

Q. What are the fears of creating results, and how should one avoid this?

A time existed during my ministry when I lost the anointing power of the Holy Spirit. The freedom and power of God's Spirit were no longer evident in my preaching.

The decline in the Spirit's anointing began near the end of my education at Stetson University. I began to coast spiritually. I gradually began to shift my dependence upon the Lord, along with my trust in the Lord, to clever methods and human ability.

I did not know it then, but as I look back now, I realize I had lost some of the glow and power I had known at first.

This decline in unction continued throughout my seminary experience at the New Orleans Baptist Theological Seminary. As a young man, I had to face the fact that Stetson was a theologically liberal college. I had some professors at Stetson and New Orleans who I thought were weak concerning the inspiration of the Scriptures. I also had some fine professors at New Orleans. However, too often I would find myself debating with them. I see now that the debating was, to some degree, impertinence wed with conviction.

I knew more in my head, but the same power from God was not in my heart. You would not have been able to prove that to me at that time. I am saying all this by reflection as I look back over my shoulder. I see for a period of time a more brash, self-assured young man who felt maybe that he had all the answers. I say this to say that theology is a wonderful thing, but it is no substitute for anointing. One could know theology and not experience the power of the Holy Spirit.

Upon graduation from New Orleans Baptist Theological Seminary, I returned to Florida and became pastor of the Park View Baptist Church in Fort Pierce. Joyce and I had meager resources as I worked our way through seminary. Our earthly possessions did not amount to much at all. I did not mind. We had each other; we had our family; we had the Lord; and we never thought of ourselves as being poor. We had no extra money to spend on anything and just did eke our way through.

Soon after we arrived on the church field, we purchased a few pieces of new furniture. It was not opulent, but we were grateful for it.

Our third child, Philip, was born shortly before we moved to the new church. As Joyce described earlier in the book, we lost Philip to SIDS on a Mother's Day afternoon. That day I had preached a sermon titled, "The Joys and Glories of the Christian Home." That afternoon, Joyce discovered Philip had stopped breathing.

On that tragic day, Joyce and I did the only thing we knew to do: turn to the Lord. When I returned home from the hospital, God directed me to 2 Corinthians 1:2-4:

> Grace be to you and peace from God our Father, and
> from the Lord Jesus Christ. Blessed be God, even the Father

of our Lord Jesus Christ, the Father of mercies, and the
God of all comfort; Who comforteth us in all our
tribulation, that we may be able to comfort them which
are in any trouble, by the comfort wherewith we ourselves
are comforted of God.

Through the reading of that Bible passage, I believed God to say,
"Adrian, I am going to give you and Joyce comfort, and I am going to
make you comforters." I was certain that the Father of mercies was going
to use this sorrow in our lives to create a blessing for other people with
broken hearts.

Joyce was standing in the doorway of our house when I returned from
the hospital without Philip. I remember looking at that new furniture
and thinking it was not only unimportant, but in the light of how much
I loved my baby, how much human life meant, thinking about eternity
and spiritual values, earthly possessions meant nothing.

The death of my son caused me to reflect and get things in sharper
spiritual focus. My life and ministerial priorities were deepened through
the death of our son. God revealed that truth to me through the experience
I had while visiting a gentleman in the hospital, that Joyce related in
chapter one.

Prior to the death of my son, I had been visiting this man. He was not
a member of my church, but he learned of the death of our baby. When I
went to see him a few days after the funeral, he said, "Are you still here?
I'm surprised to see you still serving God after what He did to you."

I said, "Sir, let me tell you this: I don't understand all that has happened,
but I want you to know that God is not the author of death. He is the
giver of life, and Satan is the thief that comes to kill, steal, and destroy.
Had there been no Satan, there would have been no sin; had there been
no sin, there would have been no death; had there been no death, I would
not have lost my son. If you think I'm going to line up with the enemy
who has hurt me, you're wrong."

God used that conversation to help sharpen my focus on eternal values. I was now a more implacable enemy of Satan. The ordeal helped heighten my desire to defeat Satan and caused me to reevaluate my relationship with the Lord.

Through the experience of Philip's death, Joyce and I began to seek the Lord in a fresh way. Near that time, Mike Gilchrist came to the church for a Bible conference. Mike taught on what it means to abide in Christ— to let Christ do in you and through you and for you what you have been trying to do for Him. Joyce and I learned afresh what it meant to abide in Christ, to be filled with the Spirit, to stop trying and start trusting. Through Gilchrist's teaching, my ministry took on a new dimension, a new focus. The Lord Jesus came into a new fullness and freshness.

I realize now that the experience of God's fullness in me that I received then was the same power I had received as a young preacher who prayed that night on the football practice field. This new dimension was really an old dimension. What I discovered then was what I had as a teenage boy—that which I did not even know how to name. I had the experience of the Holy Spirit, then gained the theology and lost the experience. Then I gained the experience back with theology, and that was the beginning of my pilgrimage of learning to depend upon the Holy Spirit.

Q. Results: Should the preacher expect them?

Not only should a pastor expect results from his pulpit ministry, but expectation should be the general tone of the pastor's ministry. A man who preaches the gospel should expect results because, based upon the evidence following the resurrection of Jesus Christ, there is not a negative note in the New Testament. Jesus said, "Ye have not chosen me, but I have chosen you, and ordained you, that ye should go and bring forth fruit" (John 15:16a). In the Old Testament, the Bible states, "the people that do know their God shall be strong, and do exploits" (Dan 11:32b). Jesus is an optimist. The writer of Hebrews says that Jesus is now sitting at God's right hand, "expecting till his enemies be made his footstool"

(Heb. 10:13b). In other words, that is the tone of Christ, and this same Christ is in you. Why should expectancy not be the preacher's tone?

Although I believe the preacher should be confident in expecting results, I would caution pastors to be careful how they measure and quantify results. Sometimes a lack of public response has caused me to experience feelings of personal failure. This was particularly true during the early years. I was convinced that a lack of public decisions for Christ was my fault. I would be so distraught that I did not want to stand at the church door following worship. I did not want to see anyone. How I wished the church had a back door so I could go out, run into the woods, and hide my shame from the people. I felt responsible. And if anyone told me it was a good sermon, it would make me angry because I believed they said it out of pity. I was tortured by the thought that if I had prayed more, or if I had prepared more, or if I were not so obtuse in my speaking, that there would have been better results.

Maturing in the Word of God allowed me to both stop condemning myself over the lack of results and to stop congratulating myself over good results. I'd describe this maturing as an ecology that one acquires from learning the battle is the Lord's and the results are His business and not the preacher's business.

Likewise I would caution preachers against the danger of expecting specific results. For years, I preached three messages each Sunday morning at Bellevue Baptist Church. The experience of preaching three messages on the same morning helped me mature in an understanding of the role of the Holy Spirit in relation to results. I came to understand that there was a mystery to preaching just as there was a mystery to the new birth.

In our old sanctuary, before we built our new one, I preached each Sunday three times back to back, 8 a.m., 9:30 a.m., and 11 a.m. I preached the same message. Sometimes at 8 heaven would come down with visible results, 9:30 would be flat, and 11 powerful again. Sometimes one service would be powerful and two services would be flat. Sometimes I would preach at 8 and ask, "I wonder if God has forsaken me? I wonder if this sermon ought to be put in the fire? I wonder what is wrong. What have I done? Where is God? What has happened?"

It was an enlightening experience to observe how differently the Holy Spirit would move in each service. The Apostle John, in the fourth Gospel, compares the Holy Spirit to a wind that "bloweth where it listeth" (John 3:8a). The first service may have had no visible decisions, yet one hour later, with the same preacher and the same sermon, there would be many decisions won for Christ.

And so I learned that it was impossible for a preacher to telegraph results. The Apostle Paul wrote, "I have planted, Apollos watered; but God gave the increase" (1 Cor. 3:6). The preacher should anticipate results, yet not demand them, for he must allow God to be God.

While the preacher should understand that God gives the increase, he cannot become indifferent concerning a lack of results.

The pastor should never make peace with the reality of preaching without results. I have heard some preachers say in regard to lack of fruit in their ministry, "I don't worry about results because that is God's concern." However, if the truth be known, the lack of results is sometimes the pastor's fault because he has been cool, diffident, and has failed to pray.

The preacher should avoid claiming the lack of results as God's doing, when, in reality, it may be his own failure. God's economy of results is much like abiding in Christ: Some pastors interpret indolence and laziness to be abiding in the Lord.

The main task of the preacher is to abide in Christ through the power of the Holy Spirit. The size of the grapes and the number of grapes are not the preacher's concern.

Q. Why should the Word of God be the preacher's primary source?

There is but one book that can speak and give us wisdom, give us knowledge, give us understanding, and give us direction. The Word of

God is not a possible source of reference material for preaching, but, rather, the primary source for preaching the gospel.

The preacher was commanded in Scripture to proclaim the Word of God. The Apostle Paul instructed Timothy to, "Preach the word; be instant in season, out of season; reprove, rebuke, exhort with all longsuffering and doctrine" (2 Tim. 4:2). The Bible is not a word merely *about* God or merely a word *from* God, but it is the Word *of* God.

There exists a difference between the knowledge of man and biblical truth. Knowledge may double but truth can never double because the Word of God is truth and it endures forever. Preachers must preach the Word of God, for God sanctifies His people through truth.

The Word of God is the source for sermons because of its inexhaustible character. The Bible can be proven to be an inexhaustible source from the fact that the Bible is relevant today. No preacher is intelligent enough to hold a congregation's interest for any extended period if he only goes to other sources for sermon material.

If you were to put the best talk-show host, comedian, lecturer, or actor in a pulpit, they could hold the attention of the people for a week, a month, or, at the best, a year. But I have been pastor at Bellevue Baptist Church for thirty-two years.

Week after week, month after month, year after year, the people would be climbing the walls to get out were this pastor drawing from his own well or making commentary on current events.

I am as excited today about my ministry here as I have ever been. Our people are excited. The source of that excitement is the Word of God.

The relevance of Scripture is one of the great affirmations that the Bible is the inerrant, inspired Word of God. The fact that here we are in the twenty-first century, preaching through a book that is millennia old attests to its inexhaustible nature.

The fact that the Bible is still relevant reveals the universality of its appeal, its effectiveness, and its supernatural inspiration. The Bible is not a book-of-the-month; it is the book of the ages.

The Word of God was settled in heaven before there were any autographs. It will be there when the earth becomes a cinder and the stars splinter and fade.

The Word of God creates freshness in each sermon, because the Bible is inexhaustible in its depth and universally applicable in its scope. In short, if the Bible is not absolute, it is obsolete. The Word of God is completely reliable.

Q. What is the impact of the inerrancy of the Word of God upon preaching?

The Bible alone is the preacher's primary source for proclaiming the gospel, for it alone is a supernatural book. Someone has well said that the Word is shallow enough to where a little child can come and get a drink without the fear of drowning, and yet it is deep enough that the theologians can swim in it forever and never touch bottom.

It is not enough to thump the Bible. It is not enough to affirm the written Word. We must proclaim the Living Word.

Although the Bible is a supernatural book, it is not automatically applicable to today's world. The Bible alone is not enough. It takes the Holy Spirit of God to open our understanding to the truth of God's Word. The preacher must study the Scriptures to determine the proper meaning of a text and then attempt to apply that truth to human needs. Scripture only has one meaning, and that is the meaning that God gave through the authors. It may have ten thousand applications, and a good preacher can take that one meaning, that one proof, whatever it is, and apply it to human hurts and needs in a multiplicity of ways.

A strong conviction of the inspiration and inerrancy of Scripture is a prerequisite if the preacher is to have authority in his message, for it is the authoritative Word that causes people to believe and behave.

Disbelief in the inerrancy of Scripture emasculates the preacher because it leaves him without authority. Liberalism and the moderate approach do not excite people. An individual would not say, "Well, praise God,

hallelujah, the Bible may be in error." Nor will they say, "Well, glory to
God, Jesus was not born of a virgin"; nor "Hallelujah, praise God, we are
not necessarily saved by the blood of Christ." Doubts do not engender
zeal and enthusiasm. People will say, "Praise God, the Bible is true;
hallelujah, Jesus was born of a virgin; thank God for the power of the
blood."

A preacher cannot declare to a congregation "this *may be* true" and
engender any real zeal. Without an infallible word from God, we have
nothing but a holy hunch, and that will not do.

Liberalism is a relative term, dependent upon where one draws the
center line of this thing called Christendom. I'd define "true inspiration"
as being convinced that all Scripture is inspired by God.

That said, I'd define a liberal Southern Baptist as a person who does
not believe in the veracity, the exactitude, the integrity, the infallibility
and inerrancy of the Scripture. Even if he believed that the Word was
inspired in its purpose but not in its entirety, he may be right of the center
in regard to Christendom but left of the center line in Southern Baptist
circles.

The moderate is a person who may believe the Bible to be without
error, but who also believes in inclusivism. He is a person who maintains
the position of accommodating the liberal view. I believe the moderate to
be more inclined to opinions than convictions.

On the other side of the spectrum, the authoritative Word engenders
conviction, which engenders zeal, and this zeal engenders church growth.

For a preacher to be powerful, he must be authoritative, and he cannot
be authoritative unless there is a sure word from God. There was a time
when preachers would stand in the pulpit, hold up the Word of God, and
say, "The Bible says." Then they started saying, "The church says." Now
they just scratch their heads and say, "Well, it seems to me."

The inerrancy of the Bible equips the preacher with authority in the
pulpit, for it supplies the preacher with the right to stand up and declare,
"Thus saith the Lord." When the Bible speaks, God speaks. That puts a

ring of authority into what the preacher has to say. The preacher is not a demagogue, he is not an authoritarian, but there is no stutter, no stammer, no apology. There is no backing away from preaching the Word. He should never be guilty of testing the temperature of the water. What the Bible says, he must say.

I am not a prophet, not an apostle, but because of the inerrancy of the Word, I can preach with the authority of a prophet or an apostle when I preach what the prophets and apostles preached.

CHAPTER

19

THE DYNAMIC OF
THE MAN OF GOD

Q. Could you speak to the necessity of the preacher's personal conversion?

The preacher's personal conversion is vital because you cannot preach what you do not know any more than you can come from where you have not been.

If the preacher has not personally received salvation, then he cannot dispense salvation. An unsaved preacher would be powerless and unprofitable in ministry, for he would be void of the power of the Holy Spirit. Yet it is possible for someone to be saved under the preaching of an un-regenerated preacher. That salvation is possible because the Word of God is the Word of God, no matter whose mouth it is in. When Balaam's donkey spoke, he was speaking on behalf of God. I do not believe the donkey was converted. There is a sense in which Paul said, "The former preach Christ from selfish ambition, not sincerely, supposing to add affliction to my chains" (Phil. 1:16, NKJ). I believe some individuals have been saved through the ministry of an unsaved preacher. An unsaved person may be a publisher of the Bible, but that does not make the Bible of non-effect.

People coming to faith through the Word of God does not mean that God has blessed the ministry of the un-regenerated preacher. Such an act by God means God has blessed His Word and demonstrated mercy upon the individual.

Q. Please discuss the importance of a call to preach.

There is a sense in which God separates a man uniquely unto Himself, and preaching may be part of that, but the gospel ministry is far larger than making an oration on Sunday morning. I would not limit the definition of the call of God upon a man to the preaching of the gospel. I view a man called of God as one who is separated unto the gospel. I often speak of my call to preach, but I am doing that out of the generally accepted usage of the term.

What I am really thinking about is something the Apostle Paul meant when he said, "Thank You, Lord, for counting me faithful, in that you put me in the ministry" (1 Tim. 1:12, author's paraphrase).

Oswald Chambers would agree. In his book *So Send I You,* he writes, "The call of God is not a call to any particular service, although my interpretation of the call may be; the call to service is the echo of my identification with God" (Christian Literature Crusade, 1973, p. 12).

Instead God's call is a call to be a man of God. I do not think a man primarily surrenders to a specific ministry, such as to preach, to teach, to sing, or to be a pastor, evangelist, or missionary. I believe he surrenders to the Lord.

Any man who is a child of God, may and should preach. I do not think there are gifted individuals who possess the oracles of God and others who do not. I think any man may and should preach if he has an opportunity. I do believe, however, that no man should be a pastor of a church or separated to the ministry who has not received a definite call.

Q. What is the importance of theological training to the preacher?

Theological training is imperative for the man called into God's ministry. I would define theology as encompassing the study of the Word of God and the study of the God of the Word.

Theological training is not necessarily synonymous with formal seminary training. A preacher may indeed receive formal theological training from a seminary. However, many seminaries are not theological training centers—though they may refer to themselves as such. *Theos* means God, and *Logos* means the Word.

Since many seminaries do not believe the Word, why should the institutions regard themselves as centers for theological training? It is like Post® Grape-Nuts® cereal, which is neither a grape nor a nut.

People ought to saturate some seminaries with their absence, because they are worse off after they attend.

I thank God for our seminaries. I believe in intellectualism. But listen to me. Our seminaries need not be elitist institutions. They need to be, primarily, incubators of a blazing, passionate, emotional love for Jesus and His Word.

The man of God must have theological training, but a preacher could acquire that knowledge while studying at his own desk. A man may never see the inside of a seminary and still be a great theologian. However, he must have a desire for the truth of God's Word and self-discipline to study.

I'd advise preachers not to preach theology. The preacher should use theology to preach Christ and not use Christ to preach theology. All theology is but the cradle in which Christ lies and the scaffolding around the building of the gospel message of Jesus. I think a lot of preachers make a mistake when they preach theology rather than use theology to preach Christ.

Q. Is rhetoric an important tool in preaching, and should it be studied?

I encourage preachers to be trained in the art of rhetoric. The preacher ought to study words. He should be a lover of words, logic, and beauty. The preacher ought to be a lover of order, and rhetoric will help him accomplish that purpose. His rhetoric ought to go beyond his words and extend into his voice and facial expressions. He should master a rhetoric that enhances his ability to communicate the Word of God.

I'd describe much of contemporary preaching as throwing mud at a wall, hoping some of it will stick. Preachers need to not only say things; they need to say things with a barb on them so the message will stick.

It might help to relate the art of rhetoric to architecture. Good architecture, like good preaching, is not just an arrangement of beautiful materials. It is a beautiful arrangement of materials. The preacher has an obligation to make his words powerful, as well as beautiful. The Bible says, "Let your speech be alway with grace, seasoned with salt" (Col. 4:6a). That is, make it palatable.

Preaching is not simply reciting words or composing a speech. One of the reasons I enjoy preaching from the King James Version of the Bible is because the translators endeavored not only to keep the objectivity and the truth of the Word, but they also endeavored to keep the rhetoric and beauty of the Word.

Q. From where does the preacher receive his authority?

The preacher's authority comes from four primary areas.

THE DIVINE CALL

The preacher's authority originates from God Himself, for all authority has its origin in God, the One who issued the call to the gospel ministry.

THE WORD OF GOD

Preachers also receive authority from the Word of God. Men have laughed at it. Men have scorned it. Men have ignored it. Men have perverted it. But it stands irrevocable. Thus the preacher stands behind the Scriptures, so he can say with a ringing affirmation, "Thus said the Lord."

RHETORICAL SKILL

Next authority is derived through the preacher's ability to make the Word of God explainable and understandable to the congregation. A preacher increases his authority by delivering a clear, articulate message from the Word of God.

PERSONAL INTEGRITY

Finally, the preacher's authority originates, in large measure, from his own personal integrity. I mention integrity last, but not necessarily because it is less important. In some ways, I could argue this source of authority should be first. The preacher's own personal integrity is imperative to his authority, for I do not believe it is possible to separate the man from his message. If the preacher is to experience real authority in the ministry, he must be the embodiment of the message that he proclaims. The man of God must submit to the Word of God and live a life of integrity, if he is to be effective in the ministry.

The preacher is to be blameless before his people. That does not mean sinless perfection. He is not sinless, but he is blameless; there is a difference. The congregation should not be able to bring an allegation upon the preacher and say that he is blameworthy in any particular area. The preacher is to be blameless in the way he lives so that the Word of God may be blameless as it is strained through his personality. I believe that a preacher of the gospel of Jesus Christ ought to aspire to be as pure as the driven snow.

Q. What is the importance of sincerity and earnestness?

Sincerity is the *sine que non* of convincing speech in preaching. Earnestness is one facet of sincerity. It is possible for a person to be earnest in what he does and yet not be sincere. I have heard of preachers who try to be sincere, but all they are is overbearing because they possess feigned sincerity. A good example is the salesman who attempts to sell magazines door-to-door. The salesman will be earnest in his attempt to sell his magazines, but he will not be sincere. He does not really care if you get the subscription to any particular magazine, or if the magazine chosen will bless your life. He only wants to make a sale.

A preacher can be earnest and not necessarily sincere at any given time during a message. The preacher must be careful not to over-emphasize sincerity in his personality, thus creating a grotesque person in the pulpit. The minister who, in order to demonstrate his sincerity, weeps and preaches with a tremor in his voice will become old and boring to the congregation.

A sincere pastor will not live a duplicitous, hypocritical life, for he would be a man who truly believes and lives the message that he preached. A sincere pastor is one who is perfectly natural. Sincerity does not mean moroseness, gravity, or heaviness. In its truest sense, it means reality— that the preacher believes and lives the message he preaches. His sincerity is self-evident.

Q. What is the importance of courage and humility?

The preacher who fears what would happen if he stood for the Lord Jesus Christ is not worth his salt as a preacher of the gospel. Courage and boldness are best observed when a preacher stands for what is right in the spirit of Christ. If there comes a time that the preacher must choose between standing for biblical truth or denying Christ and His Word, when faced with that decision, the man of God must be absolutely courageous, regardless of the cost.

The preacher must settle in his mind that the Word of God is more important than denominational approval, more important than staying in a particular church. As preachers, we do not have to stay in our denomination, we do not have to pastor our churches, we do not have to be loved. But one day we are going to give an account of our obedience to Jesus Christ, and we need to be able to say, "I was faithful to the faith; I was faithful to the fight; and I was faithful to the finish."

One of the reasons God has blessed our ministry is that I have tried to be courageous and stand for what was right, regardless of the cost. I have looked to the Lord Jesus Christ, not to Nashville, not to my deacons, not to public opinion, not to my physician, or to anything else, but I have put my eyes upon the Lord Jesus Christ. If I please Him, I'll be happy.

While I was preaching the 1986 Southern Baptist Convention sermon, I reinforced this belief: "I beg you, without stutter, without stammer, without apology, without equivocation, let us say it on television, in private, in public, and in denominational meetings that Jesus Christ is not a good way to heaven. Jesus Christ is not the best way to heaven. Jesus Christ is *the only way* to heaven."

Q. Please contrast courage and humility.

Courage and humility are inseparably wed, for the humble man without courage is a wimp, and the courageous man without humility is a bully.

I do not view courage and humility the same as brashness and self-assertiveness. Many times a pastor may believe his actions to be courageous when, in reality, his actions are crude, rude, and insensitive.

True humility is through Christ. Humility is not thinking lowly of yourself, but, rather, it is thinking about yourself from a proper biblical perspective.

Consequently, I'd define *humility* as, "Believing what God has said about you." The Bible says, "To every man that is among you, not to think of himself more highly than he ought to think; but to think soberly, according as God hath dealt to every man the measure of faith" (Rom. 12:3). Man is not to think of himself in sinful exaggeration or false humiliation, but by sober estimation. I am who the Scriptures say I am.

Many preachers confuse stooped posture for humility. Mock humility is laid upon us by none other than the devil. True humility is not thinking negatively about yourself; it is agreeing with what God says about you. The grace of God will exalt a person without inflating him and humble a person without debasing him.

Consequently, humility is not having the preacher walk around declaring how humble he is; rather, humility is having the preacher declare he is what he is by the grace of God and be willing to take the place of a servant.

Q. Please address the preacher's personal character as it relates to: work ethic, clean life, study habits, and being a student of the Bible.

A minister could easily allow himself to become a lazy preacher. If the pastor is lazy, he can deceive the congregation for a period of time by talking about the time he is spending in Bible study, prayer, and ministering to the sick and lost. Unless there is a committee that follows him around, the preacher can easily develop a poor work ethic.

In contrast, the pastoral integrity of a minister can be gauged in large measure by his work ethic. The man of God must be ethical in all areas of life, being careful that no area is so small as to avoid scrutiny.

I enjoy the ministry, and my wife playfully tells people that my hobby is preaching. I do not work myself to death, and I am not unhealthy over it. If I decide to take a day or two off, or a week off, I do not feel bad about it, because I would not hesitate to put the days, the hours, and intensity of my work up against that of any man in my congregation.

Q. What are some perils of the preacher?

Many pastors are destroyed because they allow little things to enter into their lives that later become snares and traps. The preacher's word should be his bond. He needs to be morally clean, pure in his motives, chaste in his speech, discreet in his behavior, and honest in his work ethic.

These traits do not emerge from a legalistic list of do's and don'ts. Rather, from a Christ-like character for which behavior that is intrinsically wrong becomes repugnant. It does not matter how far ahead in a race a man is; if he stops running, he will lose the race. If a preacher desires to end his ministry well, he must possess personal integrity, and that integrity must cover all areas of his life.

If you cannot be faithful in the secret things, if you cannot be faithful in the small things, God can't use you. If you are looking for a cheap way, an easy way, a lazy way to serve the Lord Jesus Christ, forget it!

CHAPTER

20

THE DYNAMIC OF
THE HOUSE OF GOD

Q. What is true worship?

Worship is basic to the Christian experience. But one man assumes a lot when he tries to tell another man how to worship. I envision the pastor as an important leader of worship and congregational worship as a key factor in effective preaching.

The dynamic of worship encompasses elements of music, praise, prayer, giving, and preaching. When we read the Word of God and preach, that is worship. When we give, that is worship. When we sing, that is worship. When we pray, that is worship. And when we fellowship, that is worship. Worship is all that I am, reacting to all that God is. In other words, I see it as doing everything in the name of the Lord Jesus and giving God the glory.

The principle of worship is not getting people saved. The bottom line is the glory of God—having people give praise to God as a result of being saved.

Q. How important is the planning of worship?

All areas related to the worship service are important and should be well-planned. I do not consider music and praise as just part of the preliminaries of worship that prepare the congregation for the main event of preaching.

Yet, I would not minimize the importance of preaching in the overall worship experience. Preaching is a key element, but not the only element, in the total worship experience. In heaven, I believe we will continue to sing and praise the Lord, but I do not know that we are going to have preaching up there.

At Bellevue Baptist Church, the minister of music has the responsibility of planning the musical aspects of congregational worship. I do not plan the music for the worship services at Bellevue. That responsibility belongs to our minister of music. He and I have worked together since 1964 and know each other well. We attempt to match the theme of the message with the music, but often neither one of us is fully prepared early enough to get it together. On these times, we let the Holy Spirit in me and the Holy Spirit in him make the two blend, and they almost always do.

Q. Please discuss the importance of praise.

Corporate worship should be designed to create an atmosphere of expectancy within the congregation. When we sing and praise God, there is created within the congregation a sense of buoyancy, a sense of victory, a sense of militancy, and a sense of expectancy. I've built this premise upon God's promise found in Psalm 22:3, which reads: "But thou art holy, O thou that inhabitest the praises of Israel." This verse I would interpret to mean that praise creates an environment in which God can interact with His people. Praise is the key mechanism to bring God dynamically present within a worship service.

Q. What is the place of Scripture reading in worship?

The public reading of the Word of God is an important element in worship. I am not opposed to a liturgical reading of the Word of God. Somehow, to me, the Scripture reading that stands alone as a part of the service, that is not related to the preaching of the Scripture is fine, provided one has an extraordinary length of time for the service. If not, I would much rather read my Scripture in conjunction with the message.

Likewise, when preaching a revival, I prefer to read my own text. Sometimes I go off to preach and a person will desire to know my sermon text so a church member could read it as part of their Scripture reading. I do not like to do that because it gets too cold between the time they read it and the time I preach it. Also, they may not read it with the inflection I desire. That's a matter of taste, but I am adamant that the Scripture ought to be read properly.

A preacher should read the Word of God carefully and meaningfully. The preacher should practice reading the Word of God privately to read well in public. The Word of God is full of drama and feeling; thus, it is crucial that it be read with feeling, proper pauses, and correct inflections. These things ought to come through the preacher's reading of the Word of God. He ought to read the Word so thoughtfully and carefully that the congregation realizes that their pastor is awed, and, therefore, they will be impressed by what he is reading.

Q. What is the proper use of public prayer?

I encourage preachers to pray short, fervent prayers that call upon God to save sinners and bless His people so His name may be glorified. Public prayer is an important element in the worship service, but I would caution against placing too much emphasis upon public prayer within the worship hour. There exists a difference between worship praying and closet praying. I do not denigrate the need for prayer. However, as I have studied the Bible, I have discovered that public prayers were relatively brief. I never do see where long prayers are glorified in Scripture. Long prayers should be expressed in our closet, and the Father who sees in secret will reward us openly (Matt. 6:6). I think sometimes we browbeat ourselves concerning enough prayer in a worship service.

Public prayer should contribute to the goal of worship which is the focused, vocal, and expressive glorifying of God. The man of God ought to come to the pulpit prayed up and not try to catch up when he gets there.

Q. What is the role of the offering in worship?

I do not view worship as distinct from the giving of tithes and offerings. The offering is a significant part of man's worship.

We receive the offering at the closing of the worship service. It is our way of saying, "God, I am giving myself to You." The money we give to the Lord represents our time, talents, and personality that has been transformed into currency. When the believer gives, he is giving a portion of himself to the Lord. People should not give from a need basis, but, rather, should give out of gratitude and love for their Lord.

CHAPTER

21

THE DYNAMIC OF PREACHING THE WORD OF GOD

Q. What is the nature and central place of preaching?

The pulpit is located in the center of the sanctuary of Bellevue Baptist Church because both the church and I deem the preaching of the Word of God to be the most important function of the church. Preaching the truth of the Word of God is imperative in building a church and a congregation. That does not mean that you can build a church with preaching alone. There are other dynamics. But you cannot build a great church without preaching.

I often have wondered, *What is the necessity of preaching? Why not give out leaflets with Scripture truths printed on them, or just mail books to people?*

Well, the nature of preaching involves a man delivering a message. I would define *biblical preaching* as applying the truth of the Bible to the human situation and calling for action. One cannot disassociate the message from the man who is preaching. Truth on paper is not the same as truth in human flesh.

The gospel message cannot be separated from the God-called messenger. A preacher once told his congregation: "I wish you did not even have to see me. The message is important; I am not important. I wish somehow there could be a curtain up here; I could stand behind the curtain, and you could just hear the message."

That man did not understand God's design for preaching. He was a hypocrite, because it would have been possible for him to preach behind a curtain if that is what he truly desired. But even if he would have constructed the curtain, that would have been contrary to God's plan. God gave him his voice; God gave him his eyes; God gave him his hands; God gave him his smile. The truth of Scripture is that God wants him out there as a chosen vessel to preach the Word of God.

Likewise, the act of hearing God's Word preached in a group setting is also crucial to the experience. Listening to a sermon alone as an individual is not nearly as powerful as listening to a sermon in a group. If you take a taped sermon and listen to that sermon while traveling in your automobile, there will be a certain chemistry that will be engendered by your listening to that tape, and you may be blessed. If something dramatic was preached, you would be moved, but only so far. However, if you were to get a group of ten people and listen to that tape, the dynamics in that room would be different. What you would hear and experience together will have greater significance than what any of you would have experienced separately.

I am not sure I understand all the psychology of that, but there is something about listening with others that builds.

Preaching is the key factor that unifies people into a congregation. If you distributed leaflets for people to read, you would just have a crowd. However, when you combine the dynamic of the crowd hearing a message at the same time and the dynamic of truth embodied in human personality, you have created something that you get through no other form of communication.

People do not only respond to the preacher, but they respond collectively one to another as they hear the message preached.

Q. Is Jesus Christ central to preaching? Why?

The preacher should never preach theology; rather, the man of God must preach the Christ of Scripture. The preacher must ask himself, *Where is Jesus in this sermon?* I believe in all of the Bible you will find Jesus. The Bible has but one hero, one villain, and one theme. The hero is Jesus, the villain is Satan, and the theme is "Jesus saves." Somehow, somewhere, in some way, that theme is present all through the Bible.

Christ is in all the Scriptures, and the Scriptures testify of Christ; Jesus is the message of the Bible and, thus, He must be the message of the preacher. The preacher should examine his message to ensure that he has preached the gospel.

Q. What is the objective of preaching?

The objective of preaching should be that people become more like Christ. The Apostle Paul wrote, "My little children, of whom I travail in birth again until Christ be formed in you" (Gal. 4:19). The measure of my ministry is not the size of our budget, the beauty of our buildings, nor the number of our attendees. The measure of my ministry is, *Are my people becoming more like Jesus Christ?*

Although I am opposed to liquor, racism, and abortion, I would not make these issues the focus of my ministry. It is easy for a preacher to become sidetracked by issues, but I determine to preach Christ and Him crucified.

Q. What is the difference between pastoral and evangelistic preaching?

Most preachers are harming their churches by overemphasizing evangelistic preaching. Pastoral preaching is not the delivery of an evangelistic sermon, but, rather, it is preaching designed to meet the needs of the congregation through a proper feeding of God's Word.

Preaching the gospel is evangelism. However, the regular worship service, led by the pastor, is not the primary place to preach the gospel. Allow me to restate my argument. Yes, preach the gospel. However, preachers who are constantly preaching, "Hell is hot, heaven is sweet, sin is black, judgment is sure, and Jesus saves" are emptying their churches because they are not feeding their sheep. Every sermon may have evangelistic overtones, and every evangelistic message may have therapeutic ideas, but the preacher must be focused in his preaching.

I do not view the preacher's love for souls as the great key that would insure ministerial success. Rather I believe the great key for ministerial success to be the preacher's personal love for Jesus Christ.

If the preacher will love Jesus, he will love what Jesus loves. Jesus asked Simon Peter, "Do you love me? Feed my sheep." Jesus did not ask, "Peter, do you love sheep, or do you love to feed sheep?" but He asked, "Do you love me? Feed my sheep."

A love for Jesus is a greater motivator than a love for people. The motivating factor behind ministry should be the preacher's desire to do something for Christ. The preacher should say in his heart, *I want to preach for Him. I want to obey Him. I want to be pleasing to Him.*

Rather than standing up before hungry sheep and explaining to them why they ought to become a sheep, the preacher should set his priority upon feeding the flock. The primary objective of church preaching is to feed the sheep.

My greatest evangelistic tool is not evangelistic preaching, but rather the ministry of people bringing the lost to Christ. Sheep who are properly fed the Word will be healthy and reproduce. I conclude virtually every message with an evangelistic appeal, but rarely would I preach a purely evangelistic message.

There is a place, from time to time, on Sunday when the pastor may desire to reap the harvest and preach a confrontational evangelistic message. Those times, in my estimation, ought to be relatively few.

Q. Is preaching God's means of spreading the gospel?

The best method to have persons respond to the message of salvation is to have sheep that will reproduce and have those sheep provoke to jealousy those who do not know the Lord Jesus Christ. Once the preacher has properly fed the sheep, he should then say to the lost, "Welcome to the table." However, if the table was not properly prepared, the lost receive a distorted picture of the gospel. Allow me to illustrate. A hungry man enters a room, and everyone is sitting down enjoying a wonderful meal.

He witnesses how they are enjoying the meal. Their joy in eating makes him desire an invitation to join in and partake of the meal. He wants to be a part of that. But if he entered the room and no one was eating and everyone wanted to force him to get the food, he would wonder what was wrong with the food.

I prefer to preach on the beauties and glories of Christ in the Christian life and at the close of the message say, "If you want to get in on that, here is how." The gospel message should provoke the lost to jealousy when they witness how Christians delight in the Lord Jesus Christ.

Q. Does preaching have a future?

I am convinced there has never been a greater date, a greater age, a greater time to preach the glorious gospel of Jesus Christ. Preaching has a future based upon the fact that the church has a future. Jesus builds His church out of saved people, and it pleased God, by the foolishness of preaching, to save them that believe; so, if the church has a future, preaching has a future.

The world is drowning in a sea of information and sinking in a swamp of degradation, filth, and meaninglessness. We are living in a day of moral fogginess where young people don't know what is right and what is wrong. The world is infested with cults that dispense deadly poison with satanic zeal. There is a militant paganism. Marching multitudes are sworn to the religion of Islam, and eastern religions are invading the shores of America.

Yet the future of preaching is bright, regardless of the world's problems because as people attempt to discover the meaning of life, the preacher will be able through the Word to provide the answer. Man has only three problems: sin, sorrow, and death; and the Bible is the only book that has the answer to those three.

God opens doors for people who are dominated by the Word of God, who are dedicated to the Son of God, who are saturated with the love of God. Behind every command of God, there is the omnipotent power of God to fulfill that command.

Let the man of God and the Spirit of God with the Word of God preach the Christ of God, and the gospel of Jesus Christ will go through the gates of hell like a white-hot cannonball through a crate of eggs.

I believe the depersonalization of human beings has created a unique opportunity for preaching to increase in effectiveness. I thank God for the Lord Jesus Christ, who gives us a name rather than a number. Contrary to popular opinion, modern forms of communication, entertainment, electronics, and computerization will not make preaching less attractive but will make preaching more attractive. People are going to be looking into so many glass eyes and computers; they are going to be so manipulated, folded, categorized, stapled, sorted, and bent that they are going to be crying out for someone with flesh and blood—someone who feels, some one who knows, someone who understands.

CHAPTER

22

SERMON
PREPARATION

Q. Explain your schedule of daily Bible reading. Is this the same as your devotional reading?

My quiet time and devotional reading time are individualized to fit my particular need. For me, prayer is the secret of fruitfulness in ministry. Most mornings begin with the sharing of a prayer and devotional time with Joyce. We read from Oswald Chamber's *My Utmost for His Highest* and other devotional materials, and pray each morning for our children, for specific needs of the church, and for a different nation of the world.

When Joyce and I have finished praying, I generally go to my study and give myself to a more serious study of the Word of God and prayer.

There are times when I enter my study and only seek the face of God in prayer. I would say that my life does not so much consist of long prayers, but, rather, of much praying. I find myself constantly praying for people. As I write letters, I pray for that person; as I read church bulletins, I pray for the pastors of those churches. The most valuable contribution a preacher can make is not when he is before his people talking about God, but when he is before God talking about his people.

Q. How important is your devotional reading in regard to helping you in general sermon preparation? What sources do you use?

My general sermon preparation and devotional readings are often the same. I have heard people say that your devotional reading needs to be one thing and your sermonic preparation needs to be something else, but I have never understood why.

If what I am preaching does not move me devotionally, in my estimation, I ought not preach it. Generally, my devotional reading is concordant with my sermon preparation.

Q. Which do you begin with first; a theme idea or a text? Why?

Once I determine that I am going to preach on a particular subject or series, I forget about anything else until I am getting near the end of that series. Then I start looking around for somewhere else to go. I really cannot give a scientific explanation of how I go from one subject to another, except by intuition, hunch, or materials that seem to appear before me that pique my interest.

I may interrupt a series of messages for a special occasion message. If I am in the middle of a series, I will parenthetically preach a special message and then resume the series.

I do place emphasis on holidays and special occasions because these times carry life and joyful expectation, which provides a unique launching pad for ideas and communication. I pay special attention to Christmas, Easter, Thanksgiving, Independence Day, and occasions within the life of the church.

Q. Explain your system of general sermon preparation (from the development of seed thoughts to gathering of material).

The preacher aims to confront, convict, convert, and comfort men and women through the preaching of biblical concepts. So, I would identify five characteristics that mark an effective sermon: it will be biblical in content, applicable, pertinent, understandable, and move to action, thus changing the individual in some constructive manner.

Preaching is more than the dissemination of truth. It is not primarily information, but transformation. It is not so much filling a bucket, as lighting a torch. The preacher is attempting to accomplish something in the hearts and minds of people. That action may be repentance, rejoicing, tithing, or soul winning.

An effective sermon moves toward effective action. If there is no call to action, there has been no sermon preached, only a lesson rendered. Some teaching is like a messenger boy who delivers a message to the front door and walks away. A sermon knocks on the front door and does not leave until it has secured an order.

A sermon should be Scriptural, understandable, persuasive, goal oriented, direct, and personal.

Q. From what sources do you derive general sermon material?

Everything is grist for the preacher's mill. I cannot give you a specific source from where I get my general sermon material, for the source comes from life itself.

For years I preached an average of six sermons per week. It seems like all my waking hours I was watching, looking, listening, making notes, or gathering materials.

I set up expandable files in my office containing some idea or theme that has caught my interest, and I begin to drop materials into those files. I may drop whole books in because there may be material in that book that I will refer to during preparation.

I may drop newspaper clippings, cards, or other sermon notes into the files. Now whether or not that information will be applicable when I read it in detail, I know not, but at least it is there so I can review it. I gather this material from everywhere just by keeping my eyes and ears open.

Q. How long should a sermon last?

The preacher should allow the occasion and subject to determine the length of the message.

A thirty-minute sermon is amply sufficient for today's society. At Bellevue, where we have multiple services on Sunday mornings, twenty-five to thirty minutes would be more than sufficient. By hard work a man could say a tremendous amount in thirty minutes or less.

Q. How important is the sermon title, and how should it be written?

The sermon title is best expressed in some rhythmic or alliterative form which catches the ear of the listener. I prepare the sermon title at the end of the sermon preparation when the title is more obvious. It should reflect clearly the message of the text and should communicate what is to be found in the sermon. The primary purpose of the title is to be descriptive of the biblical truth.

There are times when I create a title to provoke curiosity within the congregation. For example, I preached a sermon called, "Detours, Dead Ends, and Dry Holes." You would not have much idea about the real subject of the sermon, if all you knew was that title. (That sermon dealt with the pilgrimage of the Christian.) However, I have discovered that the cuter the title, the fewer the people who request the taped message.

Q. How do you construct your sermon outline?

The proper selection of a text is a matter of major significance. Good sermon preparation requires taking a passage of Scripture and analyzing it, organizing it, illustrating it, and then applying it to everyday living. The text is to be understood, believed, and applied to both personal and social needs.

Yes, it must always be a biblical text. That text may originate from Bible reading, from a series I am preaching, or from a perceived human need. When a pastor prepares a sermon, he must, in reality, or through his creative imagination, focus upon human needs, hurts, and failures.

I enjoy preaching a thematic series of messages based on the perceived needs of the congregation. If I am aware of a particular need, I will look for a text that would help me explain that particular need.

More often, though, the text is a paragraph out of an extended passage of Scripture that I am preaching through. The text commonly emerges from the series that I am preaching, and the series generally comes from a book of the Bible.

As a general rule, for exegetical preaching, a paragraph should constitute three or four verses of Scripture.

Q. As the preacher shapes his message, what should be his goal?

My sermonic goal is to discover the theme in the text and to drive that theme into the people's hearts in such a way that they would be convicted of the truth in the message and moved to action. The joy of preaching through books of the Bible is you uncover and discover themes that are fresh and relevant.

Q. How important is application of the spiritual truth to sermon preparation?

I begin sermon preparation with a specific text and allow the exegesis of the text to determine the sermon's theme. There is more than one theme that can be drawn from any text, but, almost without exception, the theme should be incipient in the text. It is important to allow the Bible to speak for itself and not try to read some thematic idea into the passage.

The sermon theme or idea begins to take shape as I study the Bible passage.

For example, one Sunday I preached on controlling the thought life or how to handle impure thoughts. This message came from the Sermon on the Mount: "Whosoever looketh on a woman to lust after her hath committed adultery with her already in his heart" (Matt. 5:28). The thematic approach was "keeping a clean thought life."

Q. How do you attempt to achieve application of spiritual truth in the message?

For a preacher to be effective, he must be able to exegete two books: God's Book and the book of human nature. I am the middle man between the Word of God and the congregation, for I must understand how to take that which is immutable, the Word of God, and apply it to that which is transitory, the human event. If the preacher does not apply the Word of God to the human event, he is only a gadfly hobnobbing with his congregation. He will never be an effective preacher. If he is cloistered behind closed doors and does not know his people, he will never be an effective preacher.

What preachers need to do is apply the Word of God to the areas of human need that exist in his congregation. The key to making it known is knowing how to apply the Word to the human situation. To do this effectively, the preacher must be aware of both worlds.

Q. What are the qualities of an effective sermon?

The work of the Holy Spirit goes before and behind the act of preaching. The Holy Spirit is involved in the preacher's sermon preparation, as well as the preacher's sermon delivery. A man does not prepare in the flesh and preach in the Spirit. He must prepare in the Spirit in order to preach in the Spirit. The Holy Spirit not only must stand with him when he preaches, but He must sit with him when he studies. The Holy Spirit must impart the truth of the Word of God to the preacher.

One key to effective sermon preparation is for the preacher to discover through the guidance of the Holy Spirit the message God desires to be preached.

As I read and study the text, there seems to arise in my heart a message that will bless and instruct my people. As I meditate on the Word of God and think of my people, the direction I need to go seems to come into my heart and mind. When a preacher examines a text, he should ask three questions:

1. WHAT DID THE TEXT MEAN THEN?

Then he must interpret it as nearly as possible to what the biblical writer meant at the time the Scripture was written.

It concerns me when I hear people say, "Isn't it wonderful how one verse of Scripture can mean so many things to so many people?" To me, that is absurdity. The text only has one meaning, and that is the meaning that God gave the original authors, nothing more, nothing less. The text needs to be interpreted in that manner.

Exegesis is designed to discover that meaning. The preacher should interpret poetry as poetry, precept as precept, parable as parable, and prophecy as prophecy.

I use critical commentaries, devotional commentaries, and word studies to uncover the meaning of the text. I encourage preachers to avoid full-set commentaries, but rather to purchase books written on a particular subject or book of the Bible. Full-set commentaries are generally weak because the writer attempts to cover too much material.

2. WHAT DOES THE TEXT MEAN NOW?

The meaning of the text has not changed, only the application of Scriptural truth. Sermonic application is achieved when the pastor discovers the application of the text, or answers the question of how the truth of the text pertains to modern life.

3. WHAT DOES THE TEXT MEAN TO ME PERSONALLY?

If you are teaching what it meant then, you may be a preacher. If you preach what it means now, you may be a preacher. But if you preach what it means to you personally, you become a prophet and a powerful preacher.

When the preacher completes all three steps, he has sharpened his focus, and his preaching becomes dynamic.

Q. Do you use cross reference Scriptures in your messages? Why?

I make use of extensive Scriptural cross-references throughout exegesis of the text.

It is a beautiful thing to bring many other Scriptures that strengthen the truth of your text. Cross referencing Scripture with your text creates an upside-down pyramid. Your text is where the point of the pyramid rests. Then, as other Scripture references are brought to bare on the text, it gets broader as you move up the inverted pyramid.

Cross referencing Scripture aides the preacher in illustrating and illuminating the truth contained in the sermon text.

Q. Text: What are its essential components?

I would describe the process of outlining the text as dividing the sermon into logical bite-size parts that adhere to the central theme of the text. The goal is for each division to stand alone and to lend credence to the theme.

I outline the passage according to the natural divisions found within the text. God gave the Bible in a natural, logical sequence, and it is the preacher's delight to discover that logical sequence. When I was a boy in Florida, I used to open coconuts. God made coconuts to have a seam on each of their three sides. A smart Florida boy knows where the seams are, and it's much easier to open a coconut along the seams.

So it is with a passage of Scripture.

Through careful study of the Word, a preacher can discover the natural division of the text.

I use an extensive outline, for it helps me to stay organized in preaching delivery and aids the listener in keeping pace with the sermon. The points in my sermon are strong enough that people can differentiate the parts of the message.

It is gratifying to me to see my people write down the points or outline of the message.

Another benefit of the sermon outline is it provides a sense of pace. Some passages do not lend themselves to a strong outline but rather flow more along a stream-of-consciousness type of preaching format. Preachers should reject forced, artificial outlines and master the art of developing strong outlines based upon the natural flow of the text.

Q. How extensive is your use of non-biblical material in sermon preparation? What sources do you use?

Once I decide on a text, exegete the text, and outline the divisions, I begin the task of incorporating non-biblical material into my specific sermon outline.

My use of non-biblical material is extensive. I think non-biblical material makes biblical material all the more interesting and applicable. People always look up, are excited, and begin to listen when contemporary issues are discussed in the light of Bible truth.

I use news magazines, newspapers, and journals as sources for non-biblical material to illustrate or apply biblical truths.

Q. How should the preacher handle the ethics of quoting material?

I would caution preachers to maintain a proper ethic when quoting another person's material. It is unethical to steal or appropriate unique material that belongs to another person.

There exist certain truths, ideas, illustrations, and thoughts that are so basic that one must stumble all over himself trying to give credit. However, there is material that is unique and original. Not to give credit for original material would be wrong.

I borrow from preachers and, in turn, they borrow from me.

I encourage preachers to strive for balance in their ethic of quoting material, for the constant quoting or giving of references can encumber the message.

Q. What qualities do you desire to include in an effective sermon?

To be effective, the pastor must preach to the needs of his people. If the preacher does not apply the spiritual truth of the text to the day in which his audience lives, the preaching becomes an exercise in futility and the church becomes a glorified country club.

The preacher should take four steps to assure spiritual application in the sermon. The preacher must first attempt to explain the truth in its biblical context. Then he must illustrate that truth and show how that truth can be applied and worked out in contemporary living. Then he must call upon his people to act upon that truth. Through application, the congregation will leave the sanctuary to live out the truth that has been preached.

One of God's great ways of communicating spiritual truth so it is easily understood is by use of illustrations. I attempt to include an illustration with every outline point of the sermon. I preplan all of my sermon illustrations through careful selection from my files.

Q. Do you write out your sermons in manuscript form? If so, why?

I do not write out my sermons in manuscript form. However, upon completion of the sermon, I do write a full outline that contains points, sub-points, and illustrations.

I take with me into the pulpit the full notes that I have made and dictated to my secretary. These notes are placed on certain size notepaper.

I highlight the key points and use these notes as my outline. It is not a manuscript, although some sections would contain full sentences in paragraph form.

I could use a shorter outline, but to me it would be double work since I have already completed the full outline.

Q. How do you structure your sermons?

I make extensive use of alliteration in my sermon outline. Alliteration is helpful, and the congregation stays on track. My mind seems to run on that track. Forced alliteration should never be used, however. Sometimes I will preach with an outline that deals with stated principles rather than briefer alliterations.

Q. How extensive is your personal library (books, audio tapes, etc.), and how much time do you spend preparing for a typical sermon?

When I begin my sermon preparation, I am drawing upon work which I have accumulated over thirty or forty years. When I begin my exegesis of a passage, I draw from my files all the materials related to that text. I have a file card on every chapter of the Bible.

This holds true of both exegesis work and illustrations. Such a filing system enables me to see what I have filed over the years on that text. Thus, when I prepare, I have available my library, my files, and, of course, my memory of the subject.

After I have assembled all the material, it requires between four to eight hours to complete a sermon.

Obviously, Wednesday night messages, and sometimes Sunday night messages, are given less time for preparation. I wish I had time to give quality time to each message, but being a busy pastor there just is not enough time for extensive preparation of each sermon.

I have hardly ever preached a message that I felt was fully ripe, fully mature before I picked it.

Q. Could you describe the importance, purpose, and content of your sermon introductions?

The introduction is vitally important and especially so when you preach to the same people year after year. The preacher should vary his introduction by posing a problem, issuing a challenge, or whetting the curiosity of the audience with a witty phrase.

I believe the introduction should be constructed after the preacher has prepared his sermon, because you cannot know what you are introducing until you have prepared the sermon.

To achieve a good sermon introduction, I recommend the formula I call, "Hey! You! Look! Do!" Each word represents an element of the introduction.

Hey! is to get their attention.

You! is where the human need enters the picture. My goal is to indicate that the subject at hand applies to the listener. This is where I say to the person whose attention I have just gotten, "I want to show you how you can get your prayers answered."

Look! is the exposition of the Scripture. My goal is to give information about the subject to come. This is where I take the Word of God and say, "Hey you, look at what the Word of God says."

Do! is where I call for action. My goal is to tell them what they are expected to do as a result of hearing the sermon. It is the "do" that makes the sermon more than just a lesson. The key function of this introduction is to secure the attention of the audience.

The preacher must take special care that the introduction actually does introduce the sermon. I generally begin by having the congregation open their Bibles to the sermon passage. Then I say, "Look up here for just a moment, and let me tell you something."

I begin to introduce the message by whatever means is appropriate for that message. The goal is to prepare the congregation for the reading of the Scripture.

The introduction requires creative thought on the part of the preacher. It must be a clear, concise opening statement. The introduction is where the preacher must focus the purpose of the sermon. He must decide what is the best way to get interest for the message. He must decide how he will make people want to listen to this message. And he must show them how the truth contained in this message will be applicable to their lives.

The objective to be achieved through the introduction is to make people determine that they will pay attention and hear what the preacher has to say.

I'd caution preachers to avoid three items in an introduction. First, avoid being so vague that the audience does not know the direction and relevance of the sermon. Second, avoid giving away too much of the sermon or the people will lose interest in the body of the message. Third, avoid spending too much time on the introduction and thus limiting the time for the rest of the sermon.

Q. How important are transitional sentences to the body of a message?

Transitional sentences are vital keys to being understood as a preacher. I use transitional sentences to create a smooth flow from one part of the sermon to the next. My transitional sentences are clear enough as to allow my people to follow along, to keep track when I move from point number one to sub-point one. A carefully constructed transition alerts the listener to the fact that I am moving from one thought to another, thus creating a smooth progression between major sections.

Q. Explain the elements and preparation of an effective conclusion.

I am concerned that preachers tend to neglect the conclusion in sermon preparation. I consider the conclusion vitally important to achieving success in preaching. It is the drawing of the net, it is getting the names signed on the dotted line.

What I desire in the conclusion is to get convictional and move peoples' hearts.

I construct the sermon conclusion through answering two questions. 1) What do I desire the people to do concerning this sermon? Answering this question ensures that the objective of the conclusion coincides with the objective of the sermon. 2) How will I move them to act upon the applied truth of the sermon?

The preacher should use variety and creativeness to achieve a solution to the second question. I enjoy concluding with a brief restatement of the important points, a dramatic illustration, or perhaps a strong challenge to the congregation.

Variety, indeed, can be given in this conclusion, but not so much as to distract the congregation from the objective of the message. The conclusion need not be long to be effective, for, in most instances, brevity is a virtue. The preacher should avoid rehashing the sermon or introducing some new thought during the conclusion.

I do end nearly every message by calling upon the people to pray with heads bowed. I would maintain a clear distinction, though, between the conclusion and the invitation. By having the congregation pray with heads bowed, I transition from the conclusion to the invitation.

Q. Would you discuss the preparation and presentation of an effective invitation?

I dedicate more preparation time to the conclusion than to the invitation. I do not prepare my invitations like the rest of the sermon. I have three or four varieties of invitations that I use and feel natural in giving without much preparation. I depend upon the inspiration of the moment rather than upon preparation for the delivery of the invitation.

In delivering an invitation, I first desire to tell the congregation what to do, then inform them what the staff will do. After this I tell them what they can say when they come forward. And, finally, I give them a word of encouragement.

The invitation I deliver in a simple style that flows naturally. I generally tell people again what it means to be saved and how they can be saved. Then I say,

> This is what I am going to ask you to do. We are going to stand and sing. The ministers of the church will be here at the front, at the head of each of these aisles. If you are willing to receive Christ as your personal Savior, I will ask you to leave your seat, come down here to the front, take

one of these ministers by the hand and tell him, "I am trusting Christ."

When you come forward, we want to go with you to a quieter place with an open Bible and show you how you can know, beyond a shadow of any doubt, that Jesus Christ is in your heart, that your sin is forgiven, and that you are ready for heaven.

We desire to treat you courteously and quietly, and I promise you on the authority of the Word of God that Jesus Christ will save you today.

I follow the same pattern for church membership and transfer of membership.

I am sure that some of my people feel this is a bit redundant, but the invitation must be extremely plain and clear to the person who is in the audience for the first or second time. Many times preachers deliver invitations that are so vague that an unsaved man would not have the foggiest idea what he is expected to do. I believe the preacher's effectiveness in the invitation is linked to his clarity, explanation, and extremely convictional delivery.

AFTERWORD

AFTERWORD:
A MESSAGE FROM
ADRIAN ROGERS

I have been given the privilege of writing this "Afterword." This is really more of a foreword. Let me explain. Our life together with our family and ministry has been an exciting book. It has been a story of God's mighty grace, remarkable victories and almost unbelievable opportunities. Of course it tells of failures and mistakes on our part. It is a book that has known sorrow and tears, yet it has been a good book.

Now we have come to the final chapter of one phase of ministry. After much struggle and prayer over the course of the last two years, I decided to retire as senior pastor of Bellevue. Let me share with you the letter of retirement I read to our congregation on September 12, 2004.

Dear Beloved Bellevue Congregation,

The grace and goodness of God brought us to serve the Bellevue Church thirty-two years ago. At that time I could have never dreamed or envisioned what God would do in these more than three decades.

As pastor and people, we have prayed together, wept together, and laughed together—all in the bond of love. When we first came to this beloved church, you opened your hearts to us and received us immediately. Your gift of love and support has sustained us through these years.

I have frequently said that when I came to Bellevue, I found in you three of the greatest qualities any pastor could hope for in a congregation. First, you believed the Bible and loved our Lord Jesus Christ. Second, you loved one another with a spirit of unity found in few churches. Last, you believed the pastor was God's anointed and appointed leader of the church.

Never have I asked you to do anything in the name of Jesus that you did not endeavor to do. Never did I have a need that you did not endeavor to meet.

The history of our time together has been recorded in heaven. This brief letter could not begin to describe the blessings and miracles we have experienced together. For thirty-two years God has heaped blessing upon blessing and victory upon victory.

God has graced Bellevue with a strong, well-trained, and gifted staff. Through the years I have leaned upon them for support, and I offer them my profound gratitude.

Our deacons and lay leadership have been beyond compare. Their unselfish service and wisdom have helped to make Bellevue the mighty church that she is.

Standing in the wings is a new generation ready to take on the challenge.

Our children and grandchildren have been nurtured and loved by you. Correspondingly, they all love Bellevue and each of you.

Now comes the time that we all knew would come when I should announce my retirement as pastor of Bellevue Baptist Church. Nevertheless, I will not retire from the ministry until I draw my last breath.

Health is not a factor in this decision. I thank God for my recovery and growing vitality and hope for many good years ahead.

Joyce and I plan to stay in Memphis and in Bellevue. We plan to continue our service to Jesus under the leadership of the new pastor.

I plan to minister through the Adrian Rogers Pastor Training Institute, which has already been set in progress. I plan to teach preaching as an adjunct professor at Mid-America Baptist Theological Seminary.

I want to continue the radio and television ministry of "Love Worth Finding." Of course, Bellevue Baptist Church, under the leadership of the new pastor, will continue to broadcast its services locally. These and other opportunities will keep me challenged and busy. I also plan to spend more quality time with my family.

Therefore, with your blessing, I offer my retirement in the spring of 2005. It is my hope that during this period a pastor search committee would be put to work. I would be thrilled to have the new pastor ready to move onto the field before or at my last days as pastor. I would love to place the baton in his hand and bless his ministry with you.

We face the future with a bright expectation of blessings upon our lives and upon this dear church. Joyce joins me in expressing our deepest love and thankfulness for these unforgettable years. To God be the glory, great things He has done!

Devotedly, your pastor

Adrian Rogers

By God's grace and the continuing strength He gives, we are beginning to write the prologue to another book. Our ministry at Bellevue as senior pastor and wife has come to an emotional but happy conclusion. It has been a good book. We will pull it many times from the shelf of our memory and turn each page with gratefulness for what God has done.

God willing, beside the radio and television ministry I'm looking forward to pouring my life and experience into the hearts and minds of young pastors.

Last, but not least, Joyce and I are looking forward to some "flex time" and quality time with each other, our four children and their mates, and our nine grandchildren.

The future is bright as long as God gives life and breath. But some day we will step through heaven's portals and begin writing one more book. That one will never have an ending.

If we may assist you in knowing
more about Jesus Christ
and the Christian life,
or if you would like to let the author know
how this book has affected your life,
please write us at:

Love Worth Finding
2941 Kate Bond Blvd.
Memphis, TN 38183-0300